THE VEG TABLE

ERIN BAKER

ISBN: 978-1-9164766-0-8

Editor: Amy Pitt | Production: Rod Shaw, Qwertyop | Photography: Mike Ruggier
Design and layout: Imogen Shaw | Indexer: Ruth Ellis

Erin Baker, founder of the Natural Cookery School, has been a professional vegetarian/vegan chef and cookery tutor for over twenty years focusing on whole food, world flavours and seasonal ingredients. She is a trained edible gardener and has a passion for edible flowers. Erin was born and bred in rural New Hampshire and currently resides in Stroud, Gloucestershire teaching at cookery schools throughout the county and further afield. Prior to living in the UK, Erin was co-owner of an award winning vegetarian restaurant in California.

Michael Ruggier is a chef, artist and food photographer, based in the South West of England. His interest in the arts informs his work across all mediums and his passion for great food, and a keen eye for detail, translate to create some truly sumptuous imagery.

For my mother
Kristine Ann Ibey
my first teacher in the kitchen
E.B.

Notes:

All spoon measurements are level unless otherwise specified.

Fruit and vegetables are medium size unless otherwise stated.

All eggs are medium size, unless otherwise stated and should ideally be free range.

Chillies are fresh, unless otherwise stated.

When a recipe calls for zest of citrus fruit, buy unwaxed fruit
or if unavailable wash well in warm soapy water before using.

Oven temperatures should be preheated to the specific temperatures.
If using a fan oven, adjust to the manufacturer's instructions.

VE means the recipe is vegan or it includes a vegan version.

GF means the recipe is gluten free or it can be made gluten free.

CONTENTS

GLOSSARY *of* INGREDIENTS

HERE IS A LIST of ingredients that you may not be familiar with or have as part of your pantry (yet!) but they are really worth getting as they will provide so much flavour and bring authenticity to your dishes.

AGAVE SYRUP
is a liquid sweetener made from the agave plant, similar to honey yet slightly more runny.

AGAR AGAR FLAKES
are a vegetarian gelatine substitute used to thicken a variety of puddings and sauces. It's made from seaweed.

AMCHOOR
is a tangy powder made from dried green mangoes used in Indian cookery.

ASAFOETIDA
also know as hing, is derived from a resin from the root of the asafoetida plant. It is used in Indian cookery and has a strong, rather unpleasant smell, but is a natural flavour enhancer and aids in digestion.

CHIPOTLE PASTE
used in Mexican cooking to add a smoky hot flavour, this paste is a blend of smoke-dried jalapeño peppers and tomatoes. Can be bought in most supermarkets.

CHINESE CABBAGE
a leafy green used in Asian cooking.

ESPAZOTE
is a Central American herb used in
Mexican cooking similar to star anise and fennel.

FLAT RICE NOODLES
are noodles made from rice found in Asian food stores.

GALANGAL
is the root of an Asian plant from the rhizome family. It can be bought at Asian food stores. Looks similar to ginger, however has a distinctly different taste.

GARAM MASALA
is a ground spice mixture used in Indian cooking.

GHEE
is butter that has been heated and strained to remove any impurities and is used in Indian cookery.

KAFFIR LIME LEAVES
a kaffir is a small lime whose fragrant leaves are often used in Asian cooking. Fresh or frozen is best, don't bother with the dried.

KECAP MANIS
is a sweet soy sauce. It's aromatic, thick and syrup. Can be found in most Asian food stores.

LEMON GRASS
is widely used in Thai cuisine, this tropical grass has a mild sweet lemony taste.

MASA HARINA
is gluten free flour made from corn. Used to make authentic Mexican tortillas, tostadas and tamales.

NIGELLA SEEDS
are small black seeds often called onion seeds.

NUTRITIONAL YEAST
is often used as a substitute for cheese in dairy free and vegan dishes due to its cheesy, creamy taste. It's a deactivated yeast so has no leavening ability. Can be bought in health food shops.

ORANGE BLOSSOM WATER/ORANGE FLOWER WATER
is made by distilling the blossoms of an orange tree. It can be bought in most supermarkets.

PALM SUGAR
this is a dark, unrefined sugar made from the sap of palm trees. It is usually grated before being added to a recipe.

SWEETENED RADISH
is preserved white radish used Southeast Asian ingredient found in most Asian food stores.

PRESERVED LEMON
is a citrusy, salty and tangy ingredient popular in North African cooking.

RAS EL HANOUT
is a fragrant North African spice mix.

RED PEPPER FLAKES
are crushed red chilli peppers, used to add spice to a dish. Aleppo chilli or pub biber do not contain seeds meaning they are a bit milder, but have a lovely flavour.

SUMAC
is a tangy, lemony spice made from the berries of a bush that grows all over the Mediterranean.

SWEET WHITE MISO
is a sweet substance made from fermented soy beans.

TAMARI
a fermented soy sauce which is often gluten free. Adds a salty dimension to a dish. When using as a substitute for soy sauce use half the amount and replace the other half with water as it is often double concentrate.

TAMARIND
is a tart fruit from the tamarind tree, used as a spice and souring agent. Can be purchased in block form and should be added to warm water to loosen then passed through a sieve to remove stones.

TAMARIND CONCENTRATE
is a tart thick syrup used in Thai cooking.

THAI BASIL
is basil native to South East Asia which as a liquorice/anise flavour. It can be bought at Asian food stores or in some supermarkets.

THAI CHILLIES/THAI CHILLI PEPPERS
also called Bird's Eye Chillies. Very spicy!

TOFU
is a nutritious curd made from soy beans and formed into blocks. It's very bland on its own but absorbs flavours really well.

TOMATILLOS
are tart green tomato like fruit used in Mexican cuisine.

WINTER SQUASH
is a squash with a hard skin that can be stored through winter. Varieties include acorn squash, butternut squash, hubbard and pumpkins.

ZA'ATAR
is a Middle Eastern spice blend containing sumac.

CONVERSION TABLES

all conversions are approximate

LIQUID MEASUREMENTS

VOLUME	UK/EUROPE	USA/CANADA
1 teaspoon	5ml	1/6 fl oz (5ml)
1 tablespoon	15ml	1/2 fl oz (15ml)
1/4 cup	60ml	2 fl oz
1/3 cup	80ml	2.5 fl oz
1/2 cup	125ml	4 fl oz
2/3 cup	160ml	5 fl oz
3/4 cup	180ml	6 fl oz
1 cup	235ml	8 fl oz

WEIGHT

METRIC	IMPERIAL
15g	1/2 ounce
30g	1 ounce
100g	3.5 ounces
115g	4 ounces
225g	8 ounces
450g	1 pound

OVEN TEMPERATURES

CELCIUS	FARENHEIT	GAS	GAS
140	275	1	cool
150	300	2	cool
170	325	3	warm
180	350	4	moderate
190	375	5	fairly hot
200	400	6	hot
220	425	7	very hot
230	450	8	very hot

INTRODUCTION

Sharing food with another human being is an intimate act that should not be indulged in lightly.

MFK FISHER

THE ROAD TO VEGETARIANISM AND VEGANISM

My childhood in rural New Hampshire was idyllic, however it left a lot to be desired from a culinary point of view, particularly for those not wanting to eat meat. Like most western households, I grew up with meat and two veg on the plate more commonly than not. Fortunately, Mom was a good cook, so was Grammie, and they both enjoyed gardening. Food was different then. There wasn't the same access to world flavours or exotic ingredients we enjoy today, and meat was a central part of what was on the plate. But we always ate healthy, home cooked, homegrown food and we ate it at the table.

I first became vegetarian as a teenager in high school; meat genuinely didn't appeal to me. Everything else on the plate was enjoyable - the veg, the sauce and the condiments. Vegetarianism was not commonplace in small-town America, leaving me little idea what it encompassed, nor did I know any vegetarians. But I knew it was something worth exploring. My first venture into being vegetarian didn't last that long, nor was it a healthy one and soon meat made its way back on to my plate.

FOOD FOR THOUGHT

While at university I became more aware of vegetarian ethics through meeting like-minded people and once again I gave up meat. In my last year I became vegan after meeting my good friend Jason. He is still vegan and has raised two healthy, bright vegan children. I spent time researching and educating myself about factory farming and animal welfare. It was the late 1990s and vegan food in America was nothing like what it is now. It was in this time and place that my thoughts of becoming a chef were first ignited. Food politics were becoming increasing important to me: I started reading labels to see what went into food. I realised that to guarantee I was eating something I was comfortable with, I needed to be cooking it myself.

After a stint volunteering with Food Not Bombs, a grass roots volunteer organisation that creates meals for the homeless out of surplus or out of date food, and a job at The Sweet Lilac Deli, a take away at a small health food co-operative in Vermont, I knew cooking was for me. The sweat of the kitchen, the pressure of service, the creativity and freedom of knowing how to cook. I loved it all. But I was vegan and did not want to go through a conventional chefs training program.

So instead I attended Bauman College, a small culinary school in Northern California. The program was focused on therapeutic healing through wholefoods and covered a range of different cuisines and alternative diet therapies. Luckily, one of my tutors attended the Culinary Institute of America, a very prestigious cookery school. She had learned the basics from the bones up, before going vegan. Together we created and owned Sparks, an award-winning vegan restaurant north of San Francisco. Here I gained a foundation in traditional cookery and was able to apply it to a career in natural, vegetarian and vegan food.

One of the first places I cut my teeth as a trained chef was at the Occidental Arts and Ecology Center in California. This remarkable place is an organic, living laboratory and has been a major influence in my life and career. For almost four years I was lucky enough to be a garden-to-kitchen chef for the center's workshops and events. Living in California also introduced me to the seed to plate mentality and the range of cultural diversity represented in food; eating locally grown ingredients that were in season and grown by farmers in the community, not far away. Alice Waters, farm to fork pioneer, became an inspiration and San Francisco awakened my palate to the infinite tastes the world has to offer.

I was vegan for about nine years, my restaurant in California was vegan and I was very active in promoting the lifestyle. Years later when I lost my mother veganism became more of a burden than the passion it once was. At the time of writing this I'm vegetarian but eat mostly plant based food. It is absolutely fabulous to see the world embracing more of a plant based lifestyle - long may it continue. Veganism is still an important part of my life, which is why most of the recipes offer a vegan variation. Food is a very personal journey and my aim is to inspire and educate you wherever you are on yours.

THE NATURAL COOKERY SCHOOL

The Natural Cookery School came into being while I was head chef at Woodruffs Organic Cafe, Britain's first totally organic cafe, in Stroud, Gloucestershire. My evening cookery classes at the cafe proved so successful starting my own school was a natural next step.

Whether I'm working at a community allotment or catering an event, delicious, healthy recipes never fail to inspire new ways of thinking about food and the way we eat day to day. It might be that someone decides to grow vegetables on their windowsill at home, go foraging, or decorate a dish with edible flowers – the Natural Cookery School is all about gaining confidence and creativity. To ultimately feel natural with ingredients and the kitchen.

BE INSPIRED

The recipes in this book are a documentation of my own culinary journey. Becoming vegan and educating myself about the food chain didn't mean submitting to a world of brown rice and broccoli. It meant being inspired by the diversity of dishes eaten every day around the world and learning how to create them at home. Most of the recipes have been inspired by my fondest food memories, whether it be dishes eaten when travelling or meals at favourite restaurants. I want to recreate these delicious sensory experiences for others.

The aim of *The Veg Table* is to offer something new: an ingredient, a knife skill, toasting of spices, making a paste or kneading of dough. Seasoned cooks will be inspired with fresh takes on familiar recipes while those just getting started in the kitchen will acquire a broad base to stand on. The recipes also show people how gorgeous vegetarian and vegan food can be.

The recipes can be cooked as is or you may find that you make a double batch of Thai green curry paste, then add a bit to your carrot soup for a touch of something special. Or a bit of leftover harissa can make a tray of roasted vegetables sing. The filling for the tamales is also wonderful as a salad with a tin of black beans thrown in. Some of my best meals at home are a combination of cookery class or catering leftovers paired with a fridge forage.

Take time to gather round the table and share meals. It is something that is lost in today's technology filled world. Make the most of vegetables; swap and change them for those in season, or maybe just avoid making moussaka in February when the aubergine won't taste as nice. Support your local farms - pay the extra for organic if you can afford it. Add your own spin to these recipes and don't be afraid to try something new. Be inspired, but most importantly, enjoy - food is one of simplest pleasures we can share with each other.

TIPS and TECHNIQUES

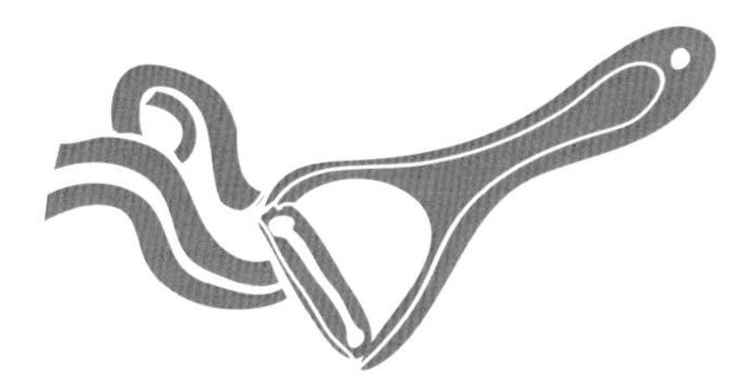

VEGETABLE PREPARATION

For any job, having the right tools is key.

PEELER

Invest in a good peeler that suits you; there are many different types and only you know which is best for you. A peeler can be used for peeling vegetables, but also for making thin ribbons of carrots, cucumbers or other vegetables for salads. I find it more effective to peel towards me rather than away.

KNIFE

A good knife does not have to be an expensive one, just one that is looked after and kept sharp. Invest in a decent knife, a steel and a sharpener or sharpening stone. A steel (long rod with a handle) will not sharpen a knife, it will only hone it, smoothing out microscopic imperfections in the blade. It is an important tool to have and I use mine daily. As far as sharpeners go, there are many out there. Go to your local kitchen shop and see what they recommend and purchase one that suits you. Sharpening stones are ideal, however most people (and chefs!) do not know how to use them properly. My favourite knives are my 8" chef's knife and my santuko Japanese style vegetable knife. If all else fails, take your knife to a local sharpener and have them restore the blade to useable condition; I do this about once a year with all my knives. Be careful as it will be very sharp when you get it back.

HAND BLENDER

Most of the recipes, if not all in this book can be done without any special equipment, besides a simple hand immersion blender. If you are able to find one that also comes with a mini chopper attachment, that is a bonus. Whenever I am buying power tools for the kitchen, I always look at engine size. Go for a hand blender that is 600W or more.

KNIFE SKILLS

Always place a wet cloth or kitchen towel under your cutting board. This creates a safe base and prevents it from moving during chopping.

SLICE

Slicing is best for most vegetables including onions and when done with a chef's knife. Create a flat, stable surface for your food to rest on by slicing it in half or slicing off a thin section of its face. Hold the food steady with your non-knife hand, curling your fingers into a claw and tucking your knuckles underneath. Hold the tip of the blade against the cutting board with the knife angled upwards, the flat side resting against your knuckles. With the tip of the blade in constant contact with the cutting board, pull the knife backwards slightly until the blade slices into the food. Continue by pressing downwards and forwards, using the full length of the blade to slice through your food. Repeat, using a circular motion and keeping the blade tip against the board at all times.

CHOP

Precision cutting of vegetables and herbs using a santoku-style knife is interchangeable with the slice, it's just a matter of style and taste (I almost exclusively chop vs. slice). You will need a very sharp knife to effectively get the chop to work without cursing your food. Create a flat, stable surface for your food to rest on by slicing it in half or slicing off a thin section of its face. Hold the food steady with your non-knife hand, curling your fingers into a claw and tucking your knuckles underneath. Hold the flat side of your knife blade against your knuckles, with the entire knife lifted above the cutting board. Press downward in a smooth, even stroke, shifting the knife forward slightly as you go. Lift the blade back up and repeat.

BACK SLICE

This technique is used for creating fine slices of small, delicate items such as herbs with minimal crushing, using either a santoku or a chef's knife. If slicing herbs, stack the leaves and roll them up into a tight bundle. Hold the food steady with your non-knife hand, curling your fingers into a claw and tucking your knuckles underneath. Place the tip of the blade against the cutting board with the flat of the blade resting against your knuckles. Hold the knife at a very low angle and pull backwards steadily, using the entire length of the blade to slice through your food, with no downward motion at all. Continue pulling backwards until the tip of your blade slices completely through the food.

ROUGH CHOP

This is ideal for finely mincing fresh herbs, zest, or other aromatics. Roughly chop your ingredients using the slice or the chop, then gather it into a small pile. Place the tip of your knife on one side of the pile and hold it steady with your free hand. Rock the knife up and down, re-gathering the ingredients occasionally, until they are as finely minced as you'd like them.

TOASTING NUTS AND SEEDS

Toasting nuts and seeds brings out the full flavour of the ingredient.

NUTS

Preheat oven to 180°C/Gas Mark 4. Place nuts on a baking tray and toast for 5-8 minutes, checking regularly and stirring until golden and fragrant.

SEEDS

Seeds can also be done in the oven or in a frying pan which is particularly effective for small seeds such as sesame. Place seeds in a dry frying pan and heat over a medium heat. Shake regularly to expose new seeds to the surface area and heat until golden, fragrant and popping sounds can be heard. Remove seeds from the pan immediately as the residual heat can burn them.

FRESH HERBS

Fresh herbs are key to maximum flavour in cooking. They are best when homegrown or purchased frequently in small quantities and can also be chopped and frozen if in danger of going off.

CORIANDER

The stem and root contain lovely intense flavour and can be added to things at the end of cooking. The leaves can be removed and roughly chopped and used to garnish.

PARSLEY

I tend to use flat leaf parsley pretty much exclusively as I prefer the flavour. The stem of parsley is often too woody to add to cooking, but makes a great handle to hold the herbs in place while chopping. Stems can be frozen and used when making vegetable stock.

MINT, BASIL, THAI BASIL, DILL AND TARRAGON

These soft herbs are best removed from the stem and carefully cut using the back slice technique or simply torn.

THYME

It can be quite labour intensive to remove thyme leaves from their stem, so try tasting a bit to see if the stem is too woody to include. When using for roasting, simply sprinkle thyme sprigs on top or if cooking on the hob, bundle together with a bit of kitchen string and add to the pot. In both cases, the leaves should fall off during the cooking process, then simply remove the stems before eating.

ROSEMARY, SAGE, BAY AND OTHER WOODY HERBS

These herbs tend to be quite intense raw and are best used when cooked. Use in small amounts and taste until you find the right balance.

LEMONS AND LIMES
Acidity plays a major role in finding the balance of flavours in dishes. When tasting a dish before serving, a little bit of lemon or lime juice can really lift flavours. Whenever I go shopping I always add two lemons and two limes to my shopping basket. If I don't end up using them in cooking, they find their way into my water or maybe something a bit stronger.

MISE EN PLACE
This is French for 'everything in place' and something that chefs do around the world to avoid mistakes when cooking on the line in a restaurant. Apply the same to your home kitchen; before you cook, have everything measured, peeled, chopped, pans greased, etc. and within reach.

SALT
Don't be afraid of salt. If you don't use much, that is fine, but do use a little and salt as you go along. I tend to use sea salt flakes.

TONGS
My favourite tool in the kitchen, they are an extension of your hand. Use them often, also great for serving salad.

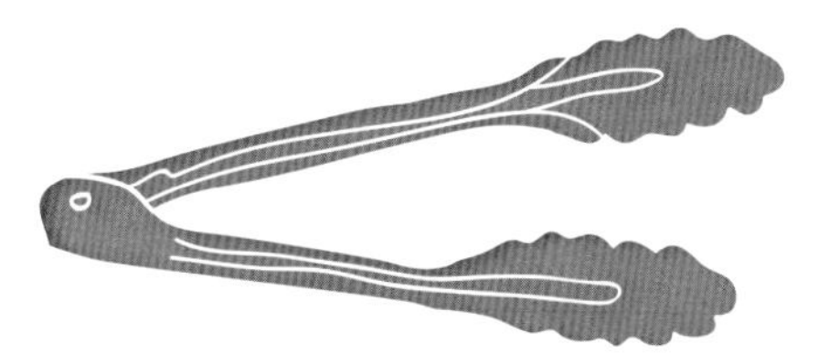

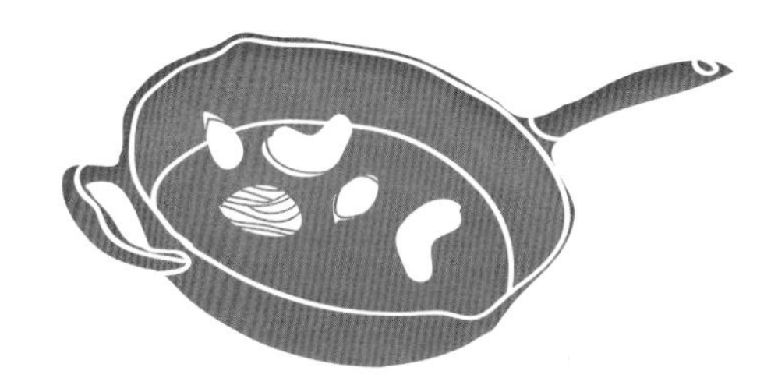

DON'T OVERCROWD YOUR PAN
When roasting or frying anything, the tendency is to cram as much in the pan as possible — resist! Do it in smaller batches instead. Crowding the pan leads to steaming and lowers the temperature of the pan so you won't get the caramelisation you're looking for — and that's where the flavour is.

CLEAN AS YOU GO
This simple tip makes a world of difference. Wipe down your cutting board in between items. Not only is it hard to chop something that is swimming in tomato juices, it's unsafe to chop on a wet surface.

DON'T FORGET THE POWER OF YOUR NOSE
If something in the oven smells done but the timer's still ticking, check on it.

TASTE AND ADJUST SEASONING
This is perhaps the single most important thing to remember. Recipes are only as good as the ingredients used. Vegetables can vary in flavour and size, and this can effect how the recipe works. Towards the end of cooking, taste and adjust seasoning. Find that perfect balance by adding a pinch of salt, a little of something sweet or something acidic to really bring the flavours together.

FLAVOURS *of the* MEDITERRANEAN

THINK WARM BEAUTIFUL SUNSHINE, salty sea air and alfresco dining. This chapter explores cuisine from countries bordering the Mediterranean Sea. There are over twenty countries surrounding this coastline, each with its own distinct dishes and flavour. The recipes in this chapter explore a few of my cookery class favourites.

One of the things I love most about Mediterranean cooking is the emphasis on people eating together with family and friends. So many of us have become removed from this with food eaten on the run or meals in front of the TV. Here cooking, eating and cleaning up is something done together.

Because Mediterranean food is primarily plant based, it makes it a natural choice for vegetarian and vegans to enjoy. Seasonal fruits and vegetables take centre stage, accentuated by whole grains, nuts, beans, pulses, fresh herbs, citrus and of course, olive oil. These recipes lend themselves to being enjoyed during the summer months, in the garden with a glass of wine.

With these recipes, use olive oil for cooking that is light in colour, not extra virgin. Extra virgin olive oil is the first press of the olive, the purest and the most flavourful; that is why it's more expensive. The second and third press from the olive provides an oil more suitable for cooking. Extra virgin has a low smoking temperature and is best used in salad dressings and as a finishing oil, drizzled over a dish before it's served. Mediterranean cultures realise this, but it's just one of many habits that so often get lost in translation when exploring different regional foods.

CAPONATA SICILIANA

I LOVE AUBERGINES. Pretty much anyway they come. Caponata has been a favourite dish of mine for decades. This recipe came from a chef at my restaurant in northern California, David, who I affectionately called Señor, not because he was Mexican, but because he was twenty years my elder and I was his boss. Thank you Señor for sharing. In true chef spirit, I'm passing it on.

Caponata is a sweet and sour aubergine based stew. It can be served warm or chilled, on bruschetta, toast, pasta, rice or even pizza. It's very versatile and can be served as a starter, main or side. I live in Stroud, Gloucestershire and we are lucky enough to have an amazing pizzeria called Fat Toni's. One of their vegetarian pizzas is caponata and I order it every time!

100ml olive oil, plus extra virgin olive oil for drizzling

3 medium aubergines, cut into 2.5cm (1 inch) cubes

2 oval shallots, thinly sliced

2-3 celery sticks, thinly sliced

4 large tomatoes, roughly chopped

3 tbsp capers, drained and roughly chopped

50g raisins or sultanas

100g green olives, pitted and sliced

50ml red wine vinegar

1 tbsp sugar

50g pinenuts

handful flat leaf parsley, chopped

salt and freshly ground black pepper

Toast pinenuts by heating a large frying pan over a medium heat. Add pine nuts and move in pan very frequently to avoid burning until fragrant and golden.

In the same frying pan, heat the olive oil and cook the aubergines with a sprinkle of salt on a moderate heat for about 15-20 minutes or until they are soft. Scoop the aubergine out of the pan with a slotted spoon. There should be some oil left in the pan.

Add the shallots and celery and cook until they are soft, stirring regularly, but not constantly, about 5-8 minutes. Add the tomatoes and cook slowly until they turn to mush. Add the cooked aubergines back to the pan along with the capers, raisins and olives. Stir well and cover. Cook for 40 minutes until all the vegetables are soft and the caponata is stew-like. Stir occasionally, but gently so the aubergines do not break up.

Mix together the red wine vinegar and sugar. Add this to the pan and cook for 10 minutes. The caponata is ready when all the vinegar has been absorbed. Season with salt and pepper, taste and adjust. Drizzle with extra virgin olive oil and stir in the pine nuts and parsley, leaving a bit for the garnish.

BLUE CHEESE, APRICOT *and* ALMOND STUFFED MUSHROOMS

STUFFED MUSHROOMS can be delicious or slightly boring. These beauties are delicious - Spanish inspired with almonds and apricots, very easy to make and even easier to pop in your mouth. Sometimes I make them with large portabello mushrooms and swap the almonds for walnuts. Either way, they are moreish, simple and quick. Serve as a main on a bed of fresh salad leaves and herb sprigs, or as a canapé.

75g almonds

15-20 small brown or chestnut mushrooms

olive oil

4 oval shallots, finely chopped

50g dried apricots, finely chopped or 2 fresh apricots, if in season, finely chopped

2 tbsp chopped fresh flat leaf parsley

100g blue cheese (Spanish if possible)

salt and freshly ground black pepper

salad leaves and herbs to serve

FOR A VEGAN VERSION
Omit blue cheese or substitute with favourite vegan alternative

Preheat oven to 180°C/Gas Mark 4 and toast almonds on a baking tray for 5-8 minutes or until fragrant and golden. Watch carefully to avoid burning. Leave to cool then finely chop by hand, with a food processor or with a nut chopper.

Remove the stems from the mushrooms by gently pressing the stem towards the edge of the mushroom. Chop the stems and set aside. Place the caps in a bowl, liberally drizzle with oil and toss until evenly coated, set aside. Heat a bit of oil in a frying pan over a medium-high heat, add the chopped mushroom stems and chopped shallots. Cook until tender.

In a mixing bowl combine the shallots, mushroom stems, chopped almonds, chopped apricots, parsley and blue cheese. Mix well and season with a pinch of salt and lots of black pepper. Divide the stuffing between the mushroom caps by lightly pressing the mixture into the base of the mushrooms. Place the mushrooms on a baking tray and bake at 200°C/Gas Mark 6 for 10-12 minutes or until tender and the cheese is bubbling.

AUBERGINE *and* LENTIL MOUSSAKA

MY HUSBAND and I got married in 2011. To keep the event simple, we had a small wedding at the registry office and then a party in a marquee at our local pub. My co-workers and I prepped all the food a couple of days before for the pub to heat and serve on the day. So yes, I did cater my own wedding and this was the main course. Everyone loved it, and a few of the meat eaters didn't even notice it was vegetarian.

A lot of people avoid cooking with aubergines due to dislike of texture, unfamiliarity or thinking that they need to salt before use. It is true that many recipes used to call for salting the aubergine before using. There are a couple of reasons for this: the first being to remove bitterness. It's my understanding that as clever humans, we have bred the bitterness out of modern aubergines and the cultivated aubergines available today are not as bitter as they used to be. The second common reason people suggest salting aubergines is to remove moisture. Some chefs recommended this delivers a better final outcome. I left behind salting aubergines decades ago and have never looked back.

Lentils provide a great replacement for mince in this recipe. I have chosen French lentils to use in this dish as they provide a wonderful texture and add a lovely flavour. Green or brown lentils could also be used.

FOR THE FILLING

4 medium or 3 large aubergines, sliced

3 tbsp olive oil

salt and freshly ground black pepper

150g Puy lentils, sometimes called dark speckled or French

1 red onion, finely chopped

1 red pepper, finely chopped

3 garlic cloves, finely chopped

2 tbsp tomato puree

400g tin chopped tomatoes

150ml red wine

1 tsp ground cinnamon

3 tbsp chopped fresh flat leaf parsley

FOR THE TOPPING

250g ricotta

250g Greek-style yoghurt

3 free-range eggs

freshly grated nutmeg

salt and freshly ground black pepper

50g freshly grated vegetarian Parmesan

FOR A VEGAN VERSION

FOR THE TOPPING:

400g silken tofu

100g cashews, soaked in hot water for 1 hour then drained

2 tbsp lemon juice

1 clove garlic

2 tsp cornflour or arrowroot

freshly ground nutmeg

salt and pepper

Combine in a blender or food processor until smooth.

Preheat the oven to 180°C/Gas Mark 4. Slice the aubergines lengthways into ½ cm (¼ inch) slices, and place on baking trays. Brush both sides with 2 tablespoons of the oil and season with salt and freshly ground black pepper. Roast until golden and floppy, about 15-20 minutes. This can be done in batches, on the barbeque or under the grill.

Put the lentils in a saucepan and cover with water - about 5cm (2.5 inch) above the lentils. Bring to a boil, reduce the heat and cook for 15-20 minutes, or until tender. Drain and rinse.

Meanwhile, in a medium size saucepan, heat the remaining tablespoon of oil, add the onion and pepper and sauté for 5-8 minutes, or until softened.

Add the garlic and tomato puree, stir to coat the vegetables, then continue to sauté for a further 4-5 minutes. Cooking the tomato puree off enhances the flavour and cooks out any bitterness.

Add the chopped tomatoes, red wine and cinnamon and simmer for 4-5 minutes.

Add the cooked lentils to the mixture and simmer for a further 2-3 minutes, or until warmed through. Add the fresh parsley and season with salt and pepper.

For the topping, in a bowl, beat together the ricotta, Greek-style yoghurt, eggs and grated nutmeg until well combined. Season with salt and pepper.

Arrange a third of the aubergines in the base of a medium size oven proof dish, and top with half the lentil mixture. Repeat, then finish with a final layer of aubergine, and top with the ricotta mixture. Sprinkle over the grated cheese. Bake at 200°C/Gas Mark 6 for about 30-45 minutes until well browned, leaving to set for 10 minutes before serving.

STUFFED TOMATOES *and* PEPPERS

STUFFED TOMATOES and peppers take me back to hot summer days in Greece travelling with my friend Sage. We had long suppers in the cool of the evening, sipping wine and enjoying the complex flavours of good ingredients cooked well, uncomplicated and unpretentious. I ordered this dish a couple of times. Traditionally the rice is put into the tomatoes and peppers uncooked, but I've saved a bit of oven time and pre-cooked the rice. I've also made it slightly healthier by reducing the copious amounts of olive oil down to a still generous amount. This is best served slightly warm or at room temperature.

4 tbsp pine nuts

12 tbsp white rice (1 tbsp per tomato or pepper, to be stuffed)

6 large ripe tomatoes

6 medium small red, yellow or orange peppers

3 tbsp olive oil

1 large onion, finely chopped

3 garlic cloves, finely chopped

small handful of fresh mint, chopped, reserving the sprigs for garnish

large handful of flat leaf parsley, chopped, reserving sprigs for garnish

1 pack of haloumi cheese, cut into very small cubes, about 0.5cm/0.25 inch

50g sultanas

200ml water

1 tbsp tomato puree

salt and freshly ground black pepper

extra virgin olive oil for drizzling

FOR A VEGAN VERSION
Omit the haloumi and replace with flavoured tofu such as basil or olive

Toast the pine nuts by heating a large frying pan over a medium heat. Add pine nuts and move in pan very frequently to avoid burning until fragrant and golden.

Preheat the oven to 200°C/Gas Mark 6

Cook the rice in a medium saucepan of boiling, salted water, stirring periodically, until almost cooked through; slightly underdone is best, about 8-10 minutes. Drain and rinse the rice under cold running water. Set aside.

Cut the tops off the tomatoes and put to one side; carefully scoop out the flesh and put to one side as well. Cut the tops off the peppers and put to one side; discard the seeds and membrane. Place the tomatoes and peppers in a roasting pan large enough to hold them comfortably.

Take the tomato flesh and process it until pureed, using a hand blender or food processor. In a bowl, combine the tomato flesh, olive oil, rice, onion, garlic, mint, parsley, nuts, cheese and sultanas and season with salt and pepper. Stuff the vegetables evenly with this mixture.

Combine the water, tomato puree and a little salt and pepper and pour this in and around the vegetables. Replace the tops of the tomatoes and peppers. Drizzle with extra virgin olive oil. Bake for 30-45 minutes. Garnish with the reserved herb sprigs.

VEGETARIAN PAELLA

PAELLA IS SUCH an attractive dish with the saffron kissed rice, fresh herbs, lemon slices and green olives. This vegetarian version is even more colourful with peppers, green beans and peas. The two key ingredients are Valencia or paella rice for the texture and smoked paprika for the complex flavour. The saffron also adds a gorgeous dimension. Saffron can be very expensive to buy in the supermarket, but is much more affordable when purchased in a world foods shop or abroad. Unless you or a loved one is planning a holiday to a Mediterranean country and can bring some back, stock up on your saffron and other spices in a shop that specializes in world foods. Saffron should never be added straight to a dish; to draw out the flavour and ensure that it is distributed throughout the dish, steep in hot stock or water first. In Spain, a good paella is judged by the 'socarrat', the crust on the bottom of the pan, so don't worry if it sticks a bit, it's going to be a winner.

¼ tsp saffron

600ml hot vegetable stock

2 tbsp rapeseed oil

2 onions, chopped

2 garlic cloves, finely chopped

1 small yellow and 1 small red pepper, seeded and sliced into rings, reserve 3 rings each

150g mushrooms, quartered

1 punnet cherry tomatoes, left whole

100g thin French green beans, trimmed and sliced in half

250g Valencia or paella rice

1 tsp paprika or smoked paprika

150ml dry white wine

125g peas, fresh or frozen and thawed

salt and freshly ground black pepper

lemon juice, to taste

extra virgin olive oil for drizzling

15-20 green olives, pitted

1 jar artichoke hearts, drained and rinsed, sliced

3 tbsp chopped flat leaf parsley

lemon wedges

Mix the saffron with the hot stock. Heat the olive oil in a large shallow frying pan or paella pan. Fry the onions gently until soft and golden. Add the garlic, peppers and mushrooms and sauté for 4-5 minutes. Then add the tomatoes and beans and cook for another 5 minutes. Season with salt and pepper. Add the rice and paprika and stir well. Pour in the white wine and bring to the boil.

Make sure the stock and saffron mixture is still very warm and pour into the pan. Reduce the heat a little and simmer for five minutes. Place the reserved pepper rings on top. Cover and reduce the heat to a simmer and cook for 15-20 minutes, or until the rice is tender. Add the peas in the last 5 minutes of cooking.

Season with lemon juice, and add salt and pepper to taste. Let stand, covered, for 5 minutes before serving. Drizzle with extra virgin olive oil, sprinkle with olives, artichoke hearts, parsley and lemon wedges.

SPINACH, SUN-DRIED TOMATO *and* GOAT'S CHEESE FRITTATA

WE USUALLY HAVE an egg dish for supper once a week. It's quick, easy and uses up what's to hand. This version showcases spinach, sun-dried tomato and goat's cheese. Other versions include roasted squash, caramelised red onion and cheddar or asparagus, pea, mint and feta. A frittata is a crustless quiche or a thick omelette with the filling mixed with the egg instead of in the middle of folded cooked egg.

2 tbsp olive oil

4 long shallots, finely chopped

200g baby spinach, or large leaf spinach chopped into smaller pieces

8 sun-dried tomatoes, chopped, or dried tomatoes reconstituted in hot water first

8 free-range eggs, beaten

small handful of fresh oregano, or 1 tsp dried

salt and freshly ground black pepper

150g soft goat's cheese

FOR A VEGAN VERSION
Omit the eggs and goat's cheese and use the ingredients below:

300ml warm water

100g chickpea flour

½ tsp salt

2 tbsp olive oil

small handful of fresh oregano, or 1 tsp dried

Preheat the oven to 180°C/Gas Mark 4. Cook the shallots in the olive oil until soft and golden in a medium frying pan that can go in the oven. If you don't have an oven proof frying pan, simply grease an oven proof dish. Add the spinach and cover until wilted. Stir in the sun-dried tomatoes. Turn off the heat.

Whisk the eggs in a bowl, add the oregano, salt and pepper. Pour this mixture over the spinach mixture in the pan. Using two spoons - one to scoop, one to scrape - dot the goat's cheese over the top. Bake for 10 -15 minutes, or until the eggs are firm. Leave to cool for about 5 minutes then cut into slices.

IF YOU ARE MAKING A VEGAN VERSION:
Place the warm water in a large bowl and sieve in the chickpea flour and salt, whisking as you go. Let sit for 2 hours or overnight. Remove any foam that has gathered on the top. Whisk in olive oil and oregano and pour into the pan at the same time the eggs would have been added.

CHOCOLATE, ORANGE & DATE CAKE
with pistachio crumble and cardamom cream

I SERVED THIS recipe at one of my Meat Free Monday's at my local pub, the Crown and Sceptre. The pub landlord, Rodda Thomas, said it was one of the best puddings he'd had in years, and he likes his puddings! I'll take that as a top mark. Thanks Rodda - and thanks too for hosting Meat Free Mondays.

FOR THE CAKE

250ml boiling water

275g dates, pitted and chopped

225g plain flour

1 tsp bicarbonate of soda

¼ tsp salt

3 tbsp cocoa powder

125g butter

200g caster sugar

2 free-range eggs

zest of 2 oranges

175g dark chocolate, broken into chunks

FOR THE CRUMBLE

75g pistachios

40g caster sugar

40g plain flour

30g chilled butter, chopped

FOR THE CREAM

100g butter, softened

200g icing sugar

1 tsp cardamom seeds, removed from the pod

200ml double cream

FOR A VEGAN VERSION

Swap butter to vegan margarine and replace each egg with 1 tbsp ground flax seed and 2 tbsp water mixed together in the cake recipe. For the crumble, replace the butter with vegan butter. For the cream, replace butter with vegan butter and the double cream with chilled coconut cream that has been drained.

Preheat the oven to 180°C/Gas Mark 4. Grease and flour a 23 x 33cm baking tray. In a small bowl, pour the boiling water over the dates and set aside to cool. In a medium bowl, mix the flour, bicarbonate of soda, salt and cocoa. Set aside.

Cream the butter and sugar together until light and fluffy. Add the eggs and orange zest. Add the flour mixture a bit at a time, alternating with the cooled date mixture. Fold in half the chocolate chunks. Pour the mixture into the prepared tray and spread evenly. Sprinkle the remaining chocolate chunks over the top. Bake for 30-35 minutes or until a cocktail stick inserted into middle of the cake comes out clean.

To make the crumble finely chop the pistachios by hand or with a food processor. Add the sugar and flour and combine. Rub the butter in with your fingers, leaving some small lumps. Line a baking tray with baking paper, tip the crumble over the tray and spread evenly. Bake for 5-7 minutes or until just golden. Set aside to cool.

To make the cream beat the butter and icing sugar together with an electric whisk or stand mixer until pale and fluffy. Add the cardamom seeds then drizzle in the cream. Continue to beat until light and airy. Do not over mix. Serve the cake with a dollop of cardamom cream and a sprinkle of pistachio crumble.

INDIAN THALI

INDIAN CUISINE covers a plethora of regional and traditional dishes from across the country. Due to its size there are many regional differences found in common recipes each one showcasing the diversity of the land, climate, occupation and cultural and religious choices. Indian cookery has developed over 8,000 years of interacting with different cultures and ingredients and the result is a diverse and varied cuisine.
To sum up India's gorgeous culinary offerings in one chapter is quite the challenge and by no means is this meant to be a definitive guide. Instead, it's a collection of some of the most popular dishes from my Indian Thali class. The word 'thali' simply means a selection of dishes served on a platter.

Asafoetida is an ingredient found in many of the recipes in this chapter. It is the dried resin of a fennel like plant grown in India and Iran. It has a strong smell and should be used in small quantities. When added to dishes is contributes a smooth flavour similar to that of leeks; it can also be used in small quantities to replace onions and garlic for those that have an intolerance or choose to avoid. It can be used as a digestive aid, flavour enhancer and a balancing agent, added to the food at the time of tempering. Tempering is the brief frying of spices in oil to release their flavour. Asafoetida can be found in most supermarkets and is a useful addition to a well stocked spice cabinet.

Simple steps to a GREAT CURRY:

Temper the oil with the spices, but be careful not to burn. The spices should be dancing around and slightly turning colour. Tempering extracts the full flavour from spices and unlocks the nutritional benefits.

Add a pinch of salt when cooking your onions and cook your onions longer than you think. This helps bring out their sweetness and will greatly effect the end result.

Add a splash of water if at any point the onions or anything else begins to stick. This releases what is caramelising onto the bottom of the pan and slightly cools down the pan.

A lower, gentle heat is better than a high hot heat.

After the onions are nice and brown, add the ginger, garlic and chilli (if using) and cook for a minute or two to release the aromatics.

When adding the dry spices be sure to have that splash (1 tablespoon) of water on hand. Cooking out your dry spices will deliver great results. Dry spices are prone to burning so this should be done with water or tomatoes in the pan. Don't be afraid of cooking your spices too much, but do be aware of cooking them too little. If you cook in a lot of oil, the oil will start to separate when the spices are cooked enough, alternatively as I don't use a lot of oil, I rely on smell. The smell of the spices changes during the cooking process. You can not over cook your spices, just be careful to not burn.

Tinned tomatoes are absolutely acceptable when fresh ripe tomatoes are not in season. The average tomato weighs 125g-150g. Simply use the equivalent of tinned chopped tomatoes.

Water, coconut milk or yoghurt can be added at the end of the cooking process to achieve the desired thickness of sauce. When adding yoghurt, make sure the heat is low otherwise it will curdle. It is still safe to eat, it just won't look as nice.

MAKES ABOUT 6 TABLESPOONS

GARAM MASALA

GARAM MASALA is used throughout Indian cuisine and as with most things it is best to make your own. It is the Indian equivalent of French herbes de Provence or Chinese five-spice powder. There are many variations on the blend throughout Indian and surrounding countries. This blend is used throughout the chapter and adds a wonderfully fragrant finish to dishes.

6-8 cardamom pods, green pods removed and discarded

2 tbsp coriander seeds

1 tbsp cumin seeds

1 tbsp black peppercorns

1 tsp whole cloves

1 tsp fennel seeds

1 7cm/3inch stick cinnamon

1 star anise

½ tsp nutmeg

Place whole spices in a dry frying pan and toast over a medium heat until fragrant, moving frequently. Transfer to a spice grinder or a mortar and pestle and grind into a fine powder.

Let cool and store in an airtight container. This will stay fresh for about six months, after that it is still good, but the flavour will start to degrade.

ONION BHAJI
with tamarind chutney

EVERYONE LOVES an onion bhaji, but my favourite part of this recipe is the tamarind chutney. It's simply divine. Make sure you purchase the tamarind that's still in a block instead of the concentrate for this recipe as it has a much better flavour. The combination of gram flour (chickpea flour) and rice flour makes for deliciously crunchy bhajis.

70g gram flour

35g rice flour

1 tbsp ghee, butter or coconut oil, melted

juice of ½ lemon

½ tsp ground turmeric

1 tsp cumin seeds, toasted and coarsely ground

½ tsp fennel seeds, toasted and coarsely ground

1 tsp garam masala

1 green chilli, seeds removed finely chopped

5cm (2 inch) fresh ginger, finely grated

2 garlic cloves, finely chopped or grated

small bunch of coriander, chopped

3 medium onions, halved, thinly sliced and core removed

salt to taste

frying oil, to cook

Sift the flours into a mixing bowl, then stir in the ghee, lemon juice, spices, ginger, garlic and fresh coriander and add salt to taste. This will produce a sandy looking mixture.

Add the onions, working them into the flour until they are well coated. Don't be afraid of squishing the onions as this will release a bit of juice helping to keep the mixture together. The mix should start to look like a paste; if it's not coming together, sparingly add a bit of water, not more than a tablespoon. The mixture should hold its shape when scooped with a spoon.

Heat about 2.5cm (1 inch) of oil in a frying pan to 180°C/Gas Mark 4 or use a wok – a drop of batter should sizzle as it hits the oil, then float. If the bhajis start to fall apart, check the oil temperature as it may be too hot or too cold. Line a plate with kitchen towel for draining the excess oil and put the oven on low.

Using a tablespoon, drop the mixture into the oil, being careful not to overcrowd the pan, then stir carefully to stop them sticking. Cook for about 6-8 minutes, turning occasionally, until crisp and golden, then drain on kitchen towel and put in the oven to keep warm while you cook the next batch. Serve with tamarind chutney.

TO SHALLOW FRY:
Form into flat patties instead of balls and fry in a little bit of oil.

TO BAKE:
Form into flat patties instead of balls and place on a greased or lined baking tray and bake in a 200°C preheated oven for 15-20 minutes or until golden.

TAMARIND CHUTNEY

100g tamarind

250ml warm water

50g dates, pitted

35g muscavado or dark brown sugar

½ tsp fennel seeds toasted and coarsely ground

½ tsp cumin seeds, toasted and coarsely ground

½ tsp salt

red chilli powder to taste

Place the tamarind in the water and let it sit for 5 minutes. Pass through a sieve with a spoon to remove the seeds and pulp. Don't forget to scrape the bottom of the sieve periodically to help more pulp pass through. Add the tamarind, dates and sugar to a saucepan and cook on a medium heat until the dates and tamarind are soft. Remove from the heat and allow the mixture to cool.

Use a food processor or hand blender to mix together into a smooth sauce. Put the sauce back into the saucepan on a medium heat and add the remaining spice ingredients. Bring the sauce to a boil and remove from the heat. Allow to cool, chill, then serve. Add salt and chilli powder to taste.

SAAG ALOO

SPINACH is one of the most versatile vegetables and it takes centre stage in this recipe. No, 400 grams of spinach is not a typo; it wilts down to almost nothing, but leaves you with a dish full of greens. It's often looked at as a side, but there's no reason why it can't be served as a main dish with rice or dhal.

4 medium potatoes

½ tbsp ground coriander

1 tsp garam masala

½ tsp ground turmeric

½ tsp ground cumin

¼ tsp asafoetida

1 tsp sugar

juice from 1 lemon
(about 3 tbsp)

4 tbsp water

3 tbsp ghee, rapeseed
or coconut oil

1 tsp mustard seeds

1 tsp cumin seeds

1 onion, thinly sliced

3 garlic cloves

2-3 fresh green chillies,
seeded and finely chopped

2.5cm (1 inch) fresh ginger,
finely grated

2 medium tomatoes,
finely chopped

400g fresh spinach, trimmed,
and roughly chopped

sea salt, to taste

Boil or bake the whole potatoes, with skins on, until a knife can be easily inserted. This is to keep in the flavour of the potato and to ensure that they are not over cooked. Remove the skin from the cooked potatoes and cut into small wedges.

In a small bowl, whisk together the spices, sugar, lemon juice and water.

Heat the ghee or oil in a large heavy bottomed non-stick skillet over a medium-high heat. When hot, add the potatoes and fry until golden brown, gently stirring often for 5-8 minutes. Remove with a slotted spoon and set aside.

Reduce the heat to medium and add the mustard and cumin seeds to the pan. Fry, stirring often, until the mustard seeds begin to dance and pop. Add the onion with a pinch of salt and cook until it starts to turn golden, adding a splash of water if it begins to stick.

Add the garlic, chillies and ginger and cook for another minute. Then add the ground spice and liquid mixture and continue to stir for another few minutes until most of the water has evaporated. Add the tomatoes and simmer for another 5 minutes or until the tomato has thickened and the liquid has evaporated.

Stir in the spinach a few handfuls at a time, until each handful is slightly wilted. Cover and simmer for about 5 minutes, stirring occasionally. Remove the lid, stir in the potatoes and season with salt. Cook for another 5 minutes to heat the potatoes through.

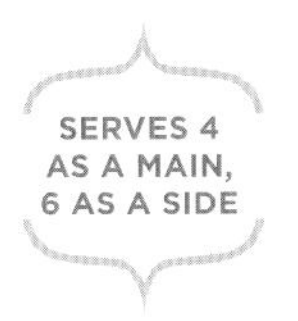

MATAR MUSHROOM
mushroom and pea curry

MUSHROOMS add great texture to vegetarian dishes and the blended cashews provide a rich creamy base for this curry. Gravy is the sauce of the curry and it's personal whether it should be thick or thin. The joy of cooking your own is you get to decide. Personally, I like a thicker gravy so I don't add too much water.

75g cashews

100ml hot water

1.25cm (½ inch) piece of ginger, peeled

2-3 garlic cloves, peeled

1 green chilli, seeds removed

2 tbsp ghee or coconut oil

1 tsp cumin seeds

¼ tsp asafoetida

1 tsp paprika

1 tsp ground coriander

½ tsp ground turmeric

salt to taste

2 medium tomatoes, cut into small pieces or pureed with a hand blender

450g fresh mushrooms, thickly sliced

200g peas, frozen or fresh

1 tsp garam masala

salt to taste

fresh coriander leaves, to garnish

To make the cashew paste, place the nuts in a bowl, cover with water and let them soak for 20 minutes. Blend or liquidize until smooth, adding more water if needed.

Make a paste with the ginger, garlic and chilli in a food processor, mortar and pestle, or chop/grate finely by hand. Heat the oil in a pan, add the cumin seeds and asafoetida. Allow the cumin seeds to splutter and turn brown, but be careful not to burn.

Add the onion with a pinch of salt and fry until it starts to turn golden, about 5-8 minutes; add a splash of water if the onion begins to stick. Stir in the ginger, garlic and chilli paste. Add the paprika, ground coriander and turmeric and stir for 30 seconds, to release the flavours.

Add the tomatoes and cook down for about 10 minutes. Add the mushrooms and cook for a few more minutes. Add the peas, stir and cook covered on a low heat. If necessary add 100ml of water. The gravy should not be too thin as mushrooms and peas let out a lot of their own water.

When the vegetables are cooked add the cashew paste, garam masala, salt to taste, and stir. Turn the heat off and allow to sit for a couple of minutes. Taste and adjust the seasoning. Garnish with chopped fresh coriander leaves.

GOBI
cauliflower curry

CAULIFLOWER is a very underrated vegetable - this curry lets it shine. Cauliflower doesn't have a strong taste, allowing it to absorb the flavours of the sauce and when cooked correctly has a great texture. An important part of cooking a curry is letting your onions cook down slowly, without burning, so don't rush this step.

2.5cm (1 inch) fresh ginger, peeled

2-3 garlic cloves, peeled

2 tbsp ghee or coconut oil

1 tsp cumin seeds

1 tsp mustard seeds

¼ tsp asafoetida

1 onion, sliced

2 medium tomatoes, chopped

½ tsp ground turmeric

1 tsp ground coriander

¼ tsp chilli powder, more to taste

1 medium cauliflower head, broken into small florets

salt to taste

100ml water

½ tsp garam masala

fresh coriander leaves, finely chopped

Make a paste with the ginger and garlic in a food processor, a mortar and pestle or chop/grate finely by hand. Heat the ghee in a pan and add the cumin seeds, mustard seeds and asafoetida. When the cumin seeds begin to splutter, add the sliced onion with a pinch of salt and cook until the onion begins to turn golden, adding a splash of water if the onion starts to stick.

Add the ginger/garlic mixture, tomatoes, turmeric, ground coriander, chilli powder, salt, and cook for 5-8 minutes or until the tomatoes start to break down. Add the small cauliflower florets and cook for a minute or two, until the vegetables look well coated and shiny. Add the water, bring to a boil and simmer for 10-15 minutes, until the cauliflower is cooked. If you like thin gravy, add more water.

Remove from the heat, add the garam masala and coriander leaves, mix gently and cover. Leave to sit for a couple of minutes. Taste and adjust the seasoning.

TARKA DHAL

DHAL SIMPLY MEANS PULSE; this explains the range of different types of dhals you can get. This recipe uses channa dhal or yellow split peas to create a creamy, velvety textured dhal. Channa dhal does take a bit longer to cook, but it's well worth the effort. Tarka means seasoning. The tarka is based on lots of garlic, cumin seeds and amchoor powder. Amchoor powder is made from dried mangos and gives a gorgeous lemony taste to the dhal. This recipe makes a lot, but it freezes well and it can also easily be halved.

200g channa dhal or yellow split peas

½ tsp turmeric

salt to taste

5cm (2 inch) fresh ginger, peeled

3 garlic cloves, peeled

1 green chilli, seeds removed

1 tbsp ghee or coconut oil

1 tsp cumin seeds

½ tsp asafoetida

1 large onion or 4 small, thinly sliced

1 tsp ground coriander

1 tsp amchoor powder, dry mango powder

fresh coriander, roughly chopped

Soak the dhal for 1 hour, then drain and rinse. Place in a pot with the turmeric and cover with 1 litre of water. Bring to a boil and skim off any scum that rises to the surface. Reduce to a simmer and cover with the lid slightly ajar. Cook until the dhal is tender, about 1-1 ½ hours, stirring occasionally. Check regularly to make sure the dhal is not sticking and add more water if needed, only a little at a time. When almost done add salt to taste. Pulses are very bland and it will take more salt than you think. Don't salt until now as this will prevent the dhal from softening.

Make a paste with the ginger, garlic and chilli in a food processor, mortar and pestle or chop/grate finely by hand. Heat a thick pan (cast iron if you have it) and melt the ghee. Add the cumin seeds and asafoetida. When the seeds start to sputter, cook carefully for a minute so as not to burn then add the onion with a pinch of salt. Cook until the onion begins to turn brown; if it starts to catch, splash with a bit of water and turn the heat down a little, this will take 10-15 minutes.

Add the ginger, garlic and chilli mixture and stir, then add the remaining dry spices, stir and cook for a minute. Remove the pan from the heat and pour over the cooked dhal. Stir in, taste and adjust the seasoning. It's traditional to stir in a spoonful of ghee when serving - I will leave that up to you. Garnish with fresh coriander.

LEMON *and* CASHEW RICE

FOR A THALI, rice that has a bit of fanciness added to it is always welcome. Lemon, cashews and a few spices dress up ordinary rice and make this dish worthy of eating on its own.

200g basmati rice

350ml water

2 tbsp ghee or coconut oil

75g cashews

½ tsp cumin seeds

½ tsp mustard seeds

handful dried or fresh curry leaves, crushed in hand

1 green chilli sliced in four long ways

½ tsp ground turmeric

salt to taste

zest and juice of 1 lemon (about 3 tbsp of juice)

Wash the rice gently, changing the water several times until the water is clear. For fluffier rice, the rice should be soaked for at least 15 minutes prior to cooking.

Drain the rice and put it into the saucepan. Add the water and salt, and bring to a boil. Once the water is boiling reduce the heat to low and cover the pan. Cook for about 15 minutes, or until the rice is tender and the water has evaporated. Rinse the rice under cold water and drain to prevent the rice from sticking. Return the rice to the cooking pan and stir in 1 teaspoon of the ghee or oil.

Heat the remaining oil in a frying pan on a medium heat; stir-fry the cashews for about 2 minutes until their colour changes to light brown. Remove the cashews with a slotted spoon and set aside. Use the same oil for rest of the seasoning.

Add the cumin seeds and mustard seeds. When the seeds start to dance around and have a party in the pan, add the curry leaves and green chilli, and stir for a few seconds. Add the turmeric and mix well.

Add the rice and cashews and sprinkle salt and lemon zest and juice all over. Mix gently, making sure not to break the rice. Stir-fry for about 2-5 minutes or until the rice is warm.

RAITA

YOGHURT is perfect for cooling the mouth down while eating curry. Removing the excess water from the cucumber and the seeds from the tomato keeps the yoghurt thick and creamy. This raita is also lovely in the summer served as a creamy salad for a barbeque.

200g thick yoghurt, Greek works well

3 tbsp fresh mint, finely chopped

salt and freshly ground black pepper to taste

½ tsp cumin seeds, toasted and coarsely ground

¼ tsp paprika

½ cucumber

1 medium tomato

FOR A VEGAN VERSION
Use vegan yogurt

In a bowl, mix the yoghurt, mint, salt, pepper, cumin seeds and paprika. Coarsely grate the cucumber. Using your hands or muslin, squeeze out the excess juice into the sink. Add to the yoghurt mixture.

Cut the tomato in half horizontally, halfway between the top and bottom, so you're not cutting through the core. Squeeze each half to remove the seeds then finely chop and add to the bowl. Combine well, taste and adjust the seasoning.

NAAN BREAD
with garlic, coriander and nigella seeds

A CURRY is not complete without a soft pillowy naan bread to mop everything up. In this recipe I have incorporated nigella seeds which are onion seeds and also know as kolanji seeds. The provide a lovely flavour and texture.

250g strong white flour

1 tsp dried active yeast

1 tsp salt

4 tbsp natural yogurt

100ml water

1 tbsp nigella seeds,
plus some for garnish

2 tbsp chopped fresh coriander

2 garlic cloves, finely chopped

melted ghee, coconut oil or
rapeseed for brushing

FOR A VEGAN VERSION
Use vegan yogurt

Measure the flour into a bowl and tip the yeast to one side and the salt to the other. Mix together the natural yogurt and water, then pour this into the flour mixture. Mix the ingredients to form a soft dough.

Turn the dough out onto a lightly floured work surface and knead for about 5-8 minutes, until it's smooth and stretchy. Gently knead in the nigella seeds, coriander and garlic.

Place the dough in a clean, oiled bowl and cover with a sheet of oiled cling film. Leave the bowl in a warm place for 1-1 ½ hours, or until it's doubled in size.

Remove the dough from the bowl and divide it into 6 pieces. You can guess, or weigh the total amount of the dough on a scale and divide by 6 or 8 depending on how big you want your naan breads, then weigh out each piece of dough accordingly.

Heat a non-stick frying pan over a very high heat and turn the oven on low. Take a piece of dough and roll it out, so it will fit in the frying pan. Pick it up by the top to stretch it slightly into a teardrop shape then place it in the hot frying pan. When the dough starts to bubble, turn it over and cook until slightly brown and not doughy. Brush with melted ghee and sprinkle with extra nigella seeds. Place in the oven to keep warm while cooking the rest.

ITALIAN KITCHEN

ITALIAN FOOD is probably the most universally known cuisine. Why is it so popular? Fresh ingredients that are simply prepared. Most recipes only have four to eight ingredients. From fresh pasta, to focaccia, to tiramisu the dishes are not complicated, but deliver full flavour. When using vegetables that are in season and high quality ingredients there's no need for elaborate preparation.

I have a poly tunnel on my allotment that I grow tomatoes and basil in. Every year, if it has been a good harvest, I make huge batches of pesto to freeze, and can homemade tomato sauce. Opening each jar, especially in February is a blast of freshness filled with memories of summer.

Fresh pasta is a wonderful thing and you should make it at least once in your life, hopefully much more. Homemade pasta just tastes that much better and has a beautiful bite and texture. Always keep the sauces simple when making fresh pasta, after all it's all about the pasta. And maybe don't try making it for the first time when your dinner guests are about to arrive, unless of course you are having them help.

Most parmesan cheese is made using animal rennet and is not vegetarian. I prefer to use one that is vegetarian. Most supermarkets carry one these days, just check the label and make sure it is suitable for vegetarians if this is a concern for you.

INSALATA CAPRESE

SIMPLE, CLASSIC AND TIMELESS. There is a reason why this salad has stood the test of time. Best made in the late summer with homegrown tomatoes and basil or purchased from a local farmer's market. Try heirloom or heritage varieties of tomatoes that offer flavour, great texture and a variety of colour.

It's also possible to make this Italian classic vegan as I discovered when I was part owner of an award-winning vegan restaurant in Northern California for a few years. Miso cured tofu with heirloom tomatoes and fresh basil was always on the menu for the summer months. Alternatively, shop bought vegan mozzarella can be used.

large, ripe vine slicing tomatoes

fresh mozzarella

large fresh basil leaves

good quality extra virgin olive oil

salt and pepper

FOR A VEGAN VERSION
Replace mozzarella with miso cured tofu:

200g block firm tofu

sweet white miso

Slice the tomatoes using a serrated knife into thick slabs about ½ cm (¼ inch).

Repeat with the mozzarella. Layer alternating slices of tomatoes and mozzarella, adding a basil leaf between each, on a large, shallow platter.

Drizzle with extra virgin olive oil and season with salt and pepper.

FOR THE MISO TOFU:
Remove the tofu from the packaging and wrap in a tea towel. Set a weight on top to release excess moisture and leave for 10 minutes. Spread a layer of miso about the size of the piece of tofu onto a plate. Place the tofu on top of the miso and frost the tofu like a cake with the miso. Make sure that the whole block is completely covered with miso and there's no tofu peeking out. Cover with a tea towel and leave out in a warm place for 2-3 days. Scrape the miso off the tofu and discard.

BRUSCHETTA

ANOTHER SIMPLE CLASSIC, but when done right - just perfect. Sweet, fresh tomatoes, fragrant basil and garlic-kissed toasted bread. Squeezing the halved tomatoes makes the mixture far less watery.

6 tomatoes or 500g cherry tomatoes

1 small red onion or ½ large onion

25g fresh basil

2 tbsp white wine, red wine, or herb vinegar

3 tbsp good quality extra virgin olive oil, plus more for brushing

salt and freshly ground black pepper

1 loaf crusty bread, preferably sourdough or ciabatta, gluten free bread is fine too

3 garlic cloves, peeled

Preheat the oven to 200°C/Gas Mark 6 or a grill to high.

Chop the tomatoes in half, from side to side, not top to bottom. Using your hand, squeeze most of the seeds out. Finish chopping the tomatoes into small pieces. Thinly slice the red onion into semi circles. Roll up the basil and thinly slice into what's called a chiffonade. Add the onion and basil to the tomatoes. Dress with the vinegar and olive oil and season with salt and pepper.

Slice the bread and lay on a baking tray. Brush with olive oil on both sides. Place in the hot oven or under the grill. Cook for 5 minutes or until just toasted, flip and cook the other side of the bread.

Remove the bread from the oven and when cool enough to touch, rub one side with garlic. Place the toasted bread on a plate and spoon on the tomato mixture. Serve immediately. Alternatively, serve the tomato mixture in a bowl and the bread on the side.

ROSEMARY FOCACCIA

I HAVE TAUGHT this focaccia recipe to hundreds of people over the years and everyone loves it. It has volumes of flavour and a big open airy crumb. Yes, you have to think ahead and start it the night before. Yes, it is messy. Yes, it has to rise twice before shaping then rise again before going in the oven. Is it really worth it? Yes, yes, yes!

Making the dough in a stand mixer is much easier, but it can be done by hand. If using a stand mixer, be careful not to over mix. It's good fun and very satisfying to knead this recipe by hand and very possible to achieve great results. We always have great fun in classes kneading the dough by hand.

This is a simple rosemary version of focaccia, but many toppings can be used. Cherry tomatoes and basil added after cooking, roasted garlic and olive, caramelised red onion and goat's cheese are just a few possibilities.

FOR THE BIGA OR SPONGE

400g strong white wheat flour

230g cool water

8g salt

a pinch of dry instant yeast (1.5g) or 3g fresh yeast

FOR THE DOUGH

600g strong white wheat flour

8g dry instant yeast (or 16g fresh yeast)

12g salt

10g sugar

500g warm water

20g good quality extra virgin olive oil, plus lots for drizzling over

20g about 4 sprigs fresh rosemary, removed from the stem and roughly chopped

coarse sea salt

Mix the sponge ingredients 12-16 hours before making the dough and leave to ferment at room temperature. This helps with the flavour, texture and crumb and is called an overnight biga.

Mix the dough ingredients, then add about three quarters of the water. Add the biga in small lumps and start kneading. If you have a suitable mixer with a dough hook, use it, because you need to develop the gluten into a very strong network in order to hold up the big gas bubbles in such a wet dough. Once you have a strong, well-developed dough that has stopped sticking to your hands or the bowl, about 10 minutes, you can gradually add the remaining water and the olive oil in very small increments. You should end up with a wet but manageable dough with a silky sheen. When finished kneading, add in about half the rosemary.

Place the dough back in the bowl. Leave covered in a warm place to rise for an hour. Tip out onto a floured surface. Gently stretch the dough and fold it back in on itself. You may need a scraper to help with this as the dough will still be quite sticky. Place it back in the bowl and leave for another hour or until doubled in size.

Preheat the oven to 240°C/Gas Mark 9. Grease two 23 x 28cm/9 x 11 inch or similar baking trays with olive oil. Tip the dough onto a heavily floured surface. Sprinkle the top lightly with flour. Cut into two equal pieces and place them on the greased baking tray. Sprinkle the surface of the dough with the remaining rosemary and coarse sea salt.

Leave covered, with greased clingfilm, in a warm place to prove for 30 minutes or until well risen. Just before baking, cover the surface of the loaves with a good glug of olive oil. To get the classic focaccia look, dip your fingers in some olive oil and dimple them into the dough several times, pushing right down to the baking tray beneath.

Bake in the oven for 20-25 minutes until golden brown. Be sure to switch the trays between racks about half way through cooking time for consistency, just don't open the oven during the first 10 minutes of baking as this is when the bread is having its final rise. Additional olive oil can be drizzled over the focaccia (and is highly recommended) after 10 minutes of baking and/or when removed from the oven. The bread is done when the centre reaches an internal temperature of 96°C. If you do not have a digital thermometer to check, ensure the bottom of the focaccia is golden and makes a hollow sound when tapped in the centre.

Place on a cooling rack to cool and although extremely tempting, do let it cool down for at least 15-20 minutes before tucking in as the bread is still cooking.

TAGLIATELLE *with pesto*

SERVES 4

HOMEMADE pasta is fun and easy to make. I always teach people that when you're making fresh pasta from scratch, keep the sauces simple and don't attempt this for the first time for a dinner party. Although it's very easy and simple to make pasta, get the hang of it first before cooking for a crowd. This is a great recipe for kids to join in with - after all, what kid doesn't like pasta?

There are two ways of salting pasta. Either salt your dough or salt your water, never salt both. I salt my water, but not my dough. I make the cooking water salty like the sea, adding 1 teaspoon of salt per litre of water. Adding oil to the cooking water is a common mistake. Never add oil to the cooking water for pasta, it may keep it from sticking together, but it also makes the sauce slip right off. In Italy, the point of eating pasta is the noodle, not the sauce. The sauce is strong and intensely flavoured and merely wrapped around the pasta. In other cultures, the pasta is drenched with sauce, disguising the beautiful pasta.

When cooking pasta, fresh or dried, reserve some of the cooking water from the pan and add to the sauce. The starches from the water help bind the sauce to the pasta. Simple and effective. Also, make sure your sauce is seasoned well.

This recipe calls for a pasta machine. Often people get them as gifts and never use them. If that is the case for you, find the pasta machine, dust it off and get it out of the box. If you don't have one, car boot sales and charity shops are great places to find ones second hand. Don't have a pasta machine? Don't fret, you can use a rolling pin. Be patient, work in small batches and give yourself plenty of space to roll it out.

Basic pasta dough

300g 00 pasta flour

3 large free-range eggs

FOR A VEGAN VERSION
Omit the egg and substitute 1 teaspoon olive oil mixed with 2 tbsp water, per egg. Add a pinch of turmeric if you would like a bit of yellow colour to the pasta.

To make the pasta, place the flour in a large mixing bowl or straight on the counter. Make a well in the middle of the flour and crack in the eggs. Using a fork, break the yolks and gently beat the eggs while incorporating the flour. When using the fork becomes difficult, switch to your hands. When the mixture comes together as a dough, turn out onto a floured surface and knead until the dough is smooth and firm. If the dough seems sticky, add a bit more flour or if it seems too dry, add a bit of water to your hands and continue kneading. Leave to rest, covered with an inverted bowl or wrapped in clingfilm for 10 minutes. The final result should basically feel like Playdough. The dough will keep in the fridge at this point for 2-3 days.

Divide the dough in two and cover one with an inverted bowl or clingfilm. Form a rough rectangle with the dough, dust with a bit of flour and feed it through the largest setting on the pasta machine. Repeat this 6-7 times, folding the dough in half, back on itself each time until the dough is smooth. The first couple of times the dough may tear and look rough, but the more it passes through, the smoother and silkier it will become. Keep the dough well-floured at all times. Repeat with the remaining dough.

Cut each sheet of pasta in two and pass through the pasta machine on the next setting down. Repeat this until the pasta is the desired thickness, switching to a lower setting each time. Each time the dough passes through the pasta machine it will get thinner and longer. It's helpful to have an assistant that catches the sheet as it comes out of the machine. If no one is around to help, make sure the dough is well-floured so it will not stick together. For tagliatelle, take the pasta to the second to last setting on the machine so there is still a good thickness. You should be able to see your hand through the sheet of pasta.

Drape the pasta over a rack or place on a floured work surface to rest for 10 minutes. This will prevent the tagliatelle from clumping. To proceed immediately into cutting, just make sure you flour the cut pasta well when finished. Attach the tagliatelle cutter to the pasta machine and feed the sheets through. Gather the strips as they come out and form loose 'nests' on a floured surface. If cutting by hand, fold the sheets of pasta and cut long strips.

Cook the pasta in a large saucepan of heavily salted boiling water for about 2-3 minutes or until al dente. Reserve a bit of the cooking liquid. Drain and return to the pan. Stir in the pesto (see the next recipe to make your own) and a tablespoon of the cooking liquid. Serve the pasta in shallow bowls and garnish with freshly grated vegetarian Parmesan.

PESTO

PESTO CAN BE MADE from a variety of herbs, flowers and greens. As this is the Italian chapter, I'm sticking with the classic, however I often make many variations. One of my favourite is nasturtium pesto in the summer with fresh nasturtium flowers and a few leaves, maybe even a few seeds pods. Cashews are a lovely nut for this variation. I also make spinach and cashew; coriander, ginger and almond; sun-dried tomato, roasted red pepper, kale and walnut. There are many variations, the key is finding the balance of the main ingredient, nuts, oil and garlic.

Shop bought pesto is affordable and readily available, so why make your own? Flavour, flavour and more flavour! While working in the production kitchen of The Organic Farm Shop in Cirencester, I processed six or seven large crates of fresh basil into pesto. By the end of the day my fingertips and nail beds had a black tint to them from all the basil leaves I'd plucked from the stems. It was great aromatherapy.

Pesto is one of my favourite things to eat at the end of summer when my poly tunnel is full of fresh basil. I try to freeze a half dozen jars or so to open in the winter and warm myself with the thought of summer sun.

The lemon juice is not entirely traditional, but I really like what it adds. Pesto made with a pestle and mortar is far superior to that done with the help of a food processor, but I will let you decide which to use. Either way, just make sure you stir in the remaining oil instead of whizzing or bashing it in. Cashews are more affordable than pine nuts and make a nice alternative.

50g pine nuts, or cashews

1 small garlic clove
(more if wanted)

salt

100g basil, leaves
only stems removed

30g vegetarian Parmesan,
finely grated

100-120ml olive oil

lemon juice to taste (optional)

FOR A VEGAN VERSION
Substitute the cheese with 2 tbsp nutritional yeast or vegan Parmesan

Heat a small frying pan over a low heat. Toast the nuts lightly, shaking regularly. Be careful not to burn, let cool.

Pound the garlic, a pinch of salt and the basil leaves in a mortar and pestle or pulse in a food processor. Add the nuts and pound again.

Turn out into a bowl and add half the grated cheese. Stir gently and add the oil, enough to bind the sauce and get a sauce consistency instead of a paste.

Season to taste, add the remaining cheese and a squeeze of lemon to finish.

WILD GARLIC PESTO

ENGLAND, IN THE SPRING, is full of wild garlic. I'm forever encouraging people to get out and take advantage of it. Wild garlic leaves are easy to recognize and if all else fails, just smell the leaves for that pungent garlic scent. There are many uses for the stuff, but pesto is very versatile and can make the most ordinary spring dish sing with flavour. Cashews are more affordable than pine nuts and make a nice alternative.

60g fresh wild garlic

30g pine nuts, lightly toasted

15g grated Italian cheese

50ml olive oil

salt to taste

lemon juice, to taste

FOR A VEGAN VERSION
Substitute the cheese with 2 tbsp nutritional yeast.

Wash and sort the wild garlic leaves. Pat dry. Place in a food processor (or beaker if using a hand blender) along with the nuts and half of the cheese. Process until finely chopped. Scrape the sides with a rubber spatula and add 2 tablespoon of the olive oil. Process again for a couple of pulses.

Place the pesto in a large bowl and stir in the remaining olive oil.

Season to taste, add the remaining cheese and a squeeze of lemon to finish.

GNOCCHI HAS A TAINTED REPUTATION due to the prepackaged varieties available in the supermarket. They are bland and very stodgy. Freshly made gnocchi should be light and fluffy like little pillows. If you're not a fan of gnocchi and have never tried freshly made, give it a go, you will be pleasantly surprised.

Gnocchi can be served as is, with a sauce of choice, or it can be pan fried in a bit of oil or butter until browned before topping with sauce, such as the fresh cherry tomato and basil ragù recipe on the next page.

Gnocchi also freezes well and can be cooked from frozen. Simply place the shaped gnocchi on a floured tray, put the tray in the freezer, and bag up when frozen – to cook when ready. The cooking time may be a minute or two longer, but when it floats, it's done.

500g potatoes

200g frozen spinach (frozen weight)

200g 00 pasta flour

Thaw the frozen spinach and squeeze out as much of the excess water as possible. Chop very finely. Boil, steam or bake the potatoes with their skins on until a knife is easily inserted. Leave to cool just a little and remove the skins while the potatoes are still warm. Use rubber gloves if the potato is too hot. Pass the warm potato through a potato ricer, grate or fluff with a fork until smooth and absolutely no lumps remain. It's very important to remove all lumps as you will feel them in the finished gnocchi.

Add the spinach and mix well. Using your hands, work the flour into the potato mixture, thoroughly, but with a light touch. When the flour has been mixed in, the dough should not be sticky or soft, it should be firm and smooth. If the dough seems sticky, add a bit more flour or if it seems too dry, add a bit of water.

Break off golf ball sizes of the dough and gently roll out into sausage-like shapes about 2.5cm (1 inch) thick. Cut the gnocchi to 2.5cm (1 inch) pieces. Touch each of the gnocchi with a fork on all sides to make grooves for the sauce. Alternatively, a gnocchi paddle can be used and is great fun. Place the gnocchi on a well-floured tray.

Cook the gnocchi in plenty of salted boiling water for just a couple of minutes. The gnocchi are ready when they float to the top. Don't cook too many at once; it's fine to reuse the water, just scoop out the floating gnocchi, bring the water back to a boil and repeat. Save a bit of the cooking water for the sauce.

FRESH CHERRY TOMATO & BASIL RAGÙ

THIS RECIPE may not be traced back to Italy, more to my restaurant in Sonoma County, California where it featured heavily in summer months. However, based on what I know about Italian cooking, I'm sure the same has been done in family kitchens across the country for centuries. Again, as with most fresh tomato based recipes, this is best done in the height of tomato season when they are affordable, available and oh so delicious.

A ragù is just an Italian name for sauce; Bolognese is a type of ragù, not to be confused with ragout, which is a thick French stew. Toss cooked gnocchi in the sauce and serve immediately with grated vegetarian Parmesan.

3-4 tbsp olive oil, not extra virgin

3-4 garlic cloves, finely chopped

600g cherry tomatoes, the orange Sun Gold variety if possible

150ml white wine

20g fresh basil, leaves only

salt and freshly ground black pepper

grated vegetarian Parmesan

FOR A VEGAN VERSION
Swap the cheese for vegan cheese

Heat a large frying pan with 3 tablespoon of olive oil over a low heat. Add the chopped garlic and gently cook for about 2 minutes, being careful not to burn otherwise the sauce will be bitter. Add the whole cherry tomatoes and stir well to lift the garlic from the bottom of the pan. Turn the heat up to medium. Cook the tomatoes for about 5 minutes, stirring regularly, adding more oil if needed. Using a potato masher or a fork, mash the cherry tomatoes. Cook for 5 more minutes then add the white wine. Reduce until most of the wine has cooked out.

Roll up the basil and thinly slice into what's called a chiffonade. Add the fresh basil and season with salt and pepper. Toss the cooked gnocchi in the sauce with a bit of the cooking liquid and gently simmer for a few minutes.

Serve immediately with grated vegetarian Parmesan.

SERVES 4

POLENTA *with mushroom ragù*

AS WITH MOST THINGS that are not cooked or seasoned properly, polenta leaves an undeserved bad taste in peoples' mouths. Yes, you can purchase pre-cooked polenta, but why would you bother when freshly made polenta is affordable, easy and quick. What's not to like? The key to making good polenta is to season it correctly. Bread would be very bland without salt, polenta is too; after all it's just coarsely ground maize. In this recipe, the polenta also gets a bit of help from butter, cheese and fresh herbs.

This recipe calls for letting the polenta set before reheating it in the oven. Alternatively, the polenta can be served soft and poured into a serving bowl when ready; in Italy, it would be like this family style, and poured straight onto a cutting board or serving dish.

FOR THE POLENTA
600ml water or vegetable stock

15g butter, at room temperature

150g quick-cooking polenta

75g vegetarian Parmesan, grated

1 tsp dried mixed herbs or 2 tbsp fresh (parsley, oregano, thyme, rosemary, basil)

salt and freshly ground black pepper

FOR THE MUSHROOM RAGÙ
2 tbsp olive oil, not extra virgin

400g chestnut mushrooms, quartered

2 onions or 1 large, finely chopped

salt and freshly ground black pepper

2 garlic cloves, finely chopped

150ml dry white wine or Marsala

150ml water or vegetable stock

1 tbsp plain flour, or rice flour for gluten free

30g butter, softened

2 tbsp chopped fresh herbs, finely chopped (parsley, oregano, thyme, rosemary, basil)

Bring the stock and butter to a boil in a heavy medium size saucepan. Gradually whisk in the polenta. As the polenta thickens it will start bubbling like lava, just be cautious. Reduce the heat to medium-low. Stir constantly until the polenta thickens, about 5 minutes.

Remove from the heat, stir in the cheese and herbs and season with salt and pepper. Pour the polenta into a greased 23 x 23cm (9 x 9 inch) or similar size baking tray, spreading so that it's 1.5cm (1 inch) thick. Cover and let stand at room temperature until set, about 30 minutes then place in the fridge for an additional 30 minutes if needed for the polenta to be firm and cool.

Meanwhile, to make the ragù, heat the oil in a large, heavy frying pan over a medium-high heat. Add the mushrooms and onion. Season with salt and pepper and sauté until the juices evaporate, about 8 minutes. Add the garlic and sauté until the mushrooms are golden brown, about 2 minutes. Reduce the heat to medium-low. Add the wine and stock. Simmer for 5 minutes or until the liquid has reduced by about half.

Stir the flour and butter in a small bowl to form a paste, then stir the paste into the mushroom mixture. Simmer until the sauce thickens slightly, about 2 minutes. Remove from the heat. Taste and adjust the seasoning.

Preheat the oven to 200°C/Gas Mark 6. Slice the now set polenta into 8 squares and then each square into a triangle and place on a greased baking tray. Heat in the oven for 10-15 minutes. Alternatively, the polenta can be pan fried in a small amount of oil. Place the heated polenta on a serving plate and top with the mushroom ragù. Sprinkle with fresh herbs.

FOR A VEGAN VERSION
Substitute the butter with vegan margarine and the cheese with 3 tbsp nutritional yeast or vegan cheese

SERVES 4-6

TIRAMISU

I'M A MASSIVE FAN of coffee and all coffee flavoured desserts. After moving to the UK I was incredibly disappointed the first time I ordered tiramisu in a restaurant. It was sponge cake, not ladyfingers and full of cream, not mascarpone. Cookery class by cookery class, I'm teaching people across the UK the correct way to make this Italian classic. There's a debate about whether or not Brandy is traditionally used as the boozy component. It was how I was taught, so therefore, that's how I make it, but if you fancy an alternative, please be my guest. And by all means make it boozier if you're so inclined.

In the summer I make a berry tiramisu by dipping the ladyfingers in elderflower cordial spiked with a fruity spirit and layer fresh fruit in the middle and on top. It's a beautiful and delicious alternative for warmer months.

3 free-range eggs

50g sugar

250g mascarpone cheese

200ml cold strong black coffee, sweetened with 2 tsp sugar when hot

2 tbsp brandy or rum

2 tbsp sweet marsala

200g Savoiardi biscuits or ladyfingers

unsweetened cocoa powder or grated dark chocolate, to decorate

Separate the eggs in a bowl. Beat the yolks and sugar until thick and creamy. Beat the whites separately until stiff with an electric mixer. Add the mascarpone to the yolk mixture, a spoonful at a time. Stir until smooth. Fold in the egg whites using a metal spoon.

Mix the coffee with the brandy and marsala in a shallow bowl. Dip half the sponge fingers in the liquid, soaking both sides and use them to line a medium size serving dish. Pour half the mascarpone mixture into the dish. Dip the remaining fingers in the liquid and arrange on top. Use the remaining mascarpone mixture to cover the top. Cover and chill for about 2 hours.

Sprinkle generously with cocoa powder or grated chocolate, before serving.

MEXICAN FIESTA

GROWING UP in New Hampshire, USA, I always loved what I thought of as Mexican food, but it wasn't until I visited Mexico and then later moved to Northern California that I developed a true passion and understanding of Mexican culture and cuisine. The country is based on the fusion of native regional cultures including Mayan, Aztec and Incan, mixed with the influence of European and African invaders. A major provider in my quest for authentic Mexican food and recipes has been Diana Kennedy, American born cookbook author and food writer, commonly referred to as the Julia Child, the Escoffier or the high priestess of Mexican cooking. Although her recipes are far from vegetarian or vegan, they tell wonderful stories, exploring native ingredients and folklore. I highly recommend any of her books for a true taste of the complexity of Mexican cuisine. The mole recipe in this chapter that I have been cooking for almost twenty years now is based on one of hers, minus the turkey stock of course.

A lot of the food we classify as Mexican is actually Tex-Mex and originated when migrant workers travelled across the border looking for work. They introduced new flavours and styles of cooking and Tex-Mex was born. I have tried to stay true to authentic Mexican, but the range of produce grown in the hot Mexican sun is a far cry from that grown here in the UK. That being said, there are fantastic Mexican grocers and online shops that make obtaining authentic ingredients achievable. Cool Chile is one of my favourite online Mexican shops and carries a range of fresh and dry ingredients.

I do hope that I have done this ancient cuisine justice in my attempt to bridge the gap between traditional Mexican and more commonly known Tex-Mex. If you asked me what my favourite cuisine is, most days I would say Mexican. You may be able to tell that by the quantity of recipes in this chapter. And I love a good tequila.

SERVES 4

TORTILLA SOUP

TORTILLA SOUP is very satisfying and soulful. This recipe is based on the traditional way to make it however I'm leaving the option to make additions like courgette, sweetcorn and beans to make the soup more of a meal. The combination of beans, sweetcorn and squash provides a hearty base for the soup, but the soup is also lovely and light without. The broken tortilla chips add texture and flavour. If making this outside squash season, courgette is a great alternative. Traditionally day old tortillas are cut into thin strips and flash fried until crunchy, however tortilla chips can also be used. Chipotles are smoked jalapeños. Chipotle paste is easy to find in big supermarkets, however if you are able to find chipotles in adobo (whole chipotles in a tomato garlic sauce) they are a great final garnish to this recipe.

6 large plum tomatoes or medium regular tomatoes

1 small onion, peeled and cut in half

4 cloves garlic, unpeeled

3 tbsp rapeseed oil

1 litre vegetable stock or water

2 tsp chipotle paste or chipotle in adobo

salt and pepper

OPTIONAL ADDITIONS

300g winter squash, cut into 2.5cm (1 inch) cubes

150g frozen sweetcorn or fresh, removed from the cob

400g tin pinto or black beans, drained and rinsed

GARNISHES

tortillas cut into thin strips and fried or tortilla chips, broken

avocado

grated cheese (optional)

fresh coriander leaves

wedges of lime

whole chipotle in adobo as a garnish

FOR A VEGAN VERSION

Use vegan cheese for garnish or omit

Heat a heavy frying pan over a medium-high heat. Add the tomatoes, peeled onion and unpeeled garlic cloves. Dry roast in the frying pan with no oil, turning regularly until the garlic is soft, about 5-8 minutes. When the garlic is soft and slightly blackened, remove from the pan and set aside to cool. Continue roasting the tomatoes and onions until charred and blackened, about 5 minutes.

Peel the garlic and place in a blender or food processor along with the charred tomatoes and onion. Blend until smooth, then pass through a sieve.

Heat the oil in a saucepan, add the sieved tomato mixture and fry until it thickens a bit, about 5 minutes. Add the vegetable stock and chipotle paste and bring to a boil. Season with salt and pepper, taste and adjust the seasoning.

At this point, any of the optional additions can be added. Cook the soup until the vegetables are tender. Otherwise, ladle into soup bowls and garnish with tortilla strips or chips, avocado, cheese, coriander and lime. A bit more chipotle paste can be added to individual bowls to make it a bit spicier if you do not have chipotles in adobo.

GUACAMOLE

EVERYONE LOVES a good guacamole! When I first moved to the UK I was shocked to see it in shops with unnecessary ingredients like yoghurt or sour cream added. As with most things, it is best to make your own. This recipe contains tomatoes, onion, jalapeño and coriander as optional ingredients. Feel free to leave them out for a simple guacamole. Quite often when I make fresh salsa at the same time as guacamole, I often leave out the optional additions. To help the garlic flavour blend in and be balanced make sure that it is very finely grated or made into a paste by finely chopping then adding a bit of salt and using the flat side of your knife to drag across the garlic until paste like.

2 large ripe avocados, removed from their skins, keep the stones

juice of ½ lime, more if needed

1 small garlic clove, made into a paste or finely grated

salt to taste

OPTIONAL ADDITIONS

1 large tomato, seeds removed

1 small red onion, finely chopped

1 jalapeño or mild green chilli, seeds removed and finely chopped

small amount of fresh coriander, finely chopped

Using a fork and a bowl or a mortar and pestle, mash the avocado, lime juice, garlic and salt together until smooth. Taste and adjust seasoning, adding more lime, salt or garlic if needed.

If using tomatoes deseed them by slicing them in half width wise so that the centre containing all the seeds is exposed. Squeeze the tomatoes to remove the majority of the seeds. Finely chop the flesh. Add remaining ingredients and stir well. Taste again and adjust seasoning if needed.

To prevent browning, if not serving immediately, place the avocado stones in the guacamole and cover with clingfilm. Make sure the clingfilm is pressed against the guacamole to prevent any oxidation as this will turn the guacamole brown. It's best served on the day it's made.

THIS RECIPE can either be chopped by hand or gently chopped in a food processor, the choice is yours, sometimes I do a bit of both. The food processor makes it more of a sauce and chopping gives it more of a salad consistency. Serve as a side with any Mexican dish or with a bowl of taco chips! Pico de gallo actually translates to the colour of the rooster's beak, which is red, just like this salsa. You will find it all over Mexico at taco stands and in restaurants. Quick, easy and the perfect condiment.

- 4 ripe tomatoes, deseeded and finely chopped
- ½ small white onion, finely chopped
- 1 jalapeno or green chilli, seeded and finely chopped
- 10g fresh coriander, chopped
- juice of ½ lime, more to taste
- salt to taste

Slice the tomatoes in half, width wise so that the centre containing all the seeds is exposed. Squeeze the tomatoes to remove the majority of the seeds. Finely chop the tomatoes. Combine all the remaining ingredients. Taste and adjust the seasoning, adding more lime, chilli or salt, if needed.

ROASTED TOMATO SALSA

WHEN TOMATOES are out of season and you must have salsa, try this one instead of a fresh salsa as the roasted tomatoes will have more flavour and a better texture. This recipe is delicious but even better when tomatoes are in season.

- 1 small red pepper, chopped into 1.25cm (½ inch) pieces
- 1 large punnet of cherry tomatoes, stems removed
- 1 small onion, finely chopped
- 1 jalapeño or green chilli, seeds removed
- 1 garlic clove, chopped
- olive oil
- 10g fresh coriander
- ½ tsp ground cumin
- juice of 1 lime
- salt and pepper to taste

Preheat the oven to 200°C/Gas Mark 6. Place the chopped red pepper, cherry tomatoes, onion, jalapeño and garlic on a baking sheet and drizzle with olive oil. Roast for 10-15 minutes. When done, place in a bowl and add the remaining ingredients. Pulse in a food processor or with a hand blender for a chunky consistency. Taste and adjust the seasoning.

SALSA VERDE

SALSA VERDE is one of my favourite salsas, not to be confused with the Spanish version that contains parsley and capers. The Mexican version is made from tomatillos, a round fruit that is green when ripe and has an outer husk like its cousin physalis. I first discovered tomatillos while living in Northern California. A regular customer at my restaurant, Terry, had grown far too many in his vegetable garden and asked me if I would like some. I had eaten them many times, but never cooked with them. I graciously accepted the challenge and produced over a dozen jars of salsa verde for my cupboard. Every year I grow tomatillos on my allotment as they are very hard to find in this country, also I am greedy and like to have enough to make a big batch of salsa verde to preserve in jars to have throughout the year. Thank you Terry for the inspiration that has stayed with me.

It is possible to find tomatillos in the UK. A few online shops periodically carry them, along with local farmer's markets. Have a look or try growing your own if space allows. Seeds are readily available online. Salsa verde is great to eat as a dip for tortilla chips, and lovely as a sauce on soft tacos, or enchiladas.

400g fresh tomatillos, husks removed and halved if large

2 jalapeños or mild green chillies, seeded and chopped

2 small onions, roughly chopped

4 garlic cloves

rapeseed oil

25g of fresh coriander

1 lime, juice only

salt and sugar to taste

Preheat the oven to 200°C/Gas Mark 6. Place the tomatillos, chillies, onions and garlic on a baking sheet. Drizzle with oil and toss to coat. Roast for about 20 minutes or until beginning to brown. Remove from the oven and place in a bowl.

Add the coriander and lime juice to the bowl and puree using a hand blender until mostly smooth. Taste and add salt and sugar if needed.

PINK PICKLED ONIONS

PINK PICKLED ONIONS are from the Yucatan. The flavour is perky as well as the colour, adding to the taste and appearance of Mexican dishes. Use as a garnish for soft tacos, enchiladas, or on top of beans and rice. My husband often exclaims "why don't you make these more often" when I have them left over from a class and tops anything he is eating with them until the jar is gone.

2 medium red onions, halved and thinly sliced

good pinch of ground cinnamon

3 whole cloves

pinch of crushed red pepper flakes

125ml cider or white wine vinegar or enough to cover the onions

½ tsp salt

Add the sliced red onions to a medium bowl and pour enough boiling water over them so they are covered. Count to 10 then drain.

Put the onions along with the rest of the ingredients into a glass jar and combine gently, pressing the onions down so that the liquid covers the onions. Put the lid on the jar and leave to sit until the onions go bright pink, 2-3 hours. The onions will keep for about 5-7 days in the fridge.

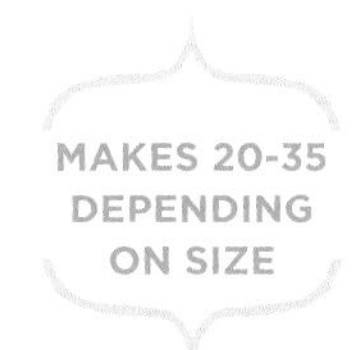

CORN TORTILLAS

MASA HARINA is nixtamalized corn flour made from maize that's soaked in lime and ash to remove the outer husk. This adds flavour to the maize and aids in the digestion of nutrients found in the grain. It's the staple ingredient of soft corn tortillas and tamales. Masa harina and corn husks can be ordered online from Mexican grocery stores.

Soft corn tortillas are used for soft tacos or enchiladas and can be fried for crispy taco shells or tortilla chips. They are a staple Mexican ingredient and are found everywhere in Mexico and throughout the United States, but are very hard to get hold of in the UK. Solution? Make your own. Corn tortillas are naturally gluten free.

250g masa harina

330ml hot tap water

In a large bowl combine the masa harina with the hot water to form a dough. Leave covered with clingfilm or a tea towel for 15 minutes. Knead in more water if necessary; the texture should be like soft clay but not sticky.

To form the tortillas, pinch off a piece of dough and roll into a ball. Have a little pot of cold water nearby to dip your fingertips into when rolling if the dough feels a little dry. 15g balls make 8-10cm tortillas and 25-30g balls make 12-15cm tortillas.

Place the dough ball between two sheets of clingfilm (two plastic bags also work well) and either roll out into a 3mm thick circle with a rolling pin or use a tortilla press. If using a tortilla press, press once then turn 180 degrees and repeat. Peel the plastic off the top of the tortilla, then place the uncovered side of the tortilla in your palm and, at an angle, carefully remove the other piece of plastic. The best way to make the tortillas is to shape and then place right on a hot pan. Otherwise place tortillas on a tray lined with parchment, but do not stack.

In a dry, very hot frying pan, gently place your tortilla and cook for 30 seconds or until the tortilla releases itself from the pan. Turn over and cook the other side for 30-45 seconds. Turn once more. Hopefully the tortilla will puff; you can help it along by gently pressing the edges with a spatula when you see a bubble forming. Don't worry if it does not, just look for small specs of brown to appear. Have a folded clean tea towel by the side and as you make the tortillas tuck them in the tea towel to keep them warm.

PORTABELLO MUSHROOM FAJITAS

FAJITAS trace back to Mexican ranch workers living across the border in Texas. Does that make it Mexican or Tex-Mex? You decide. Either way fajitas are great. This vegetarian version is made with meaty portabello mushrooms. Don't leave the mushrooms to marinate too long, as they start to break down and won't have as nice a texture.

4 large portabello mushrooms, sliced into 2.5cm (1 inch) thick strips

1 large onion, halved and thinly sliced

1 small red pepper, halved and thinly sliced

1 small yellow or orange pepper, halved and thinly sliced

FOR THE MARINADE

juice of 1 lime, more to taste

2 tsp chipotle paste

1 tsp ground cumin

2 tbsp rapeseed or olive oil

pinch of black pepper

pinch of salt

small handful of fresh coriander

rapeseed oil for cooking

pack of flour or corn tortillas, or homemade (see previous recipe)

TO SERVE

fresh salsa

guacamole

Preheat the oven to 200°C/Gas Mark 6.

Firstly, chop the vegetables and set aside. Make the marinade in a large bowl by combining all the ingredients. Add the vegetables to the marinade and toss well. Let everything sit for about 15 minutes to soak up the flavours. Taste the marinade and add more chipotle paste if desired. Wrap the tortillas in kitchen foil and warm in the oven for 8-10 minutes.

Place a frying pan over a medium-high heat and add some oil. When hot, quickly cook the marinated vegetables in small batches for about 5 minutes, or until the onions and pepper are tender. Place the cooked vegetables in a hot oven to keep warm. Serve the vegetables with the warm tortillas along with fresh salsa and guacamole.

ROASTED SQUASH *and* MANGO SOFT TACOS

IN MEXICO, the cheeses are very subtle and creamy, unlike the punchy cheddars we have in the UK. Feta may seem a weird choice, but it works well; opt for a creamy feta instead of a salty or long cured one. Wensleydale is also a good substitute for Mexican cheese. In the summer, swap the squash for sweetcorn, it's delicious! Simply strip the corn off the cob carefully using a knife and then roast for about 10 minutes or until starting to colour.

1 small or ½ large butternut squash or similar winter squash

2 tbsp olive oil

salt and pepper

100g mild feta, or Wensleydale

zest and juice of 1 lime

1 jalapeño or green chilli, seeds removed and finely chopped

10g fresh coriander, finely chopped (about 3 tbsp)

2-4 spring onions, thinly sliced

12 corn tortillas, shop bought or homemade (see recipe)

1 ripe mango, peeled, halved, pit removed and sliced into 12 long strips

lime wedges, to serve

FOR A VEGAN VERSION
omit the cheese altogether or use a vegan feta

Preheat the oven to 200°C/Gas Mark 6. Place the whole squash in the oven for 10 minutes to soften, making it easier to peel and chop. Let cool. Peel the squash, cut in half lengthways and scoop out the seeds. Slice into small 1.25cm (½ inch) cubes. Drizzle with 1 tablespoon of oil, season with salt and pepper and roast for 15-20 minutes.

Meanwhile combine the feta, lime zest, lime juice, remaining oil, jalapeño, coriander and spring onions in a bowl. Add the squash to the bowl when roasted. Season with salt and pepper, taste and adjust the seasoning.

Wrap the tortillas in kitchen foil and heat for 10 minutes in a hot oven. Alternatively, place them in a dry (no oil) frying pan over a medium heat and cook them for about 15 seconds on each side. You can also do away with the frying pan and char the tortillas directly over the gas flames for a few seconds using tongs!

To serve, place a spoonful of the squash mixture on the tortilla and top with a mango slice and serve with lime wedges.

SWEET POTATO AND CORN TAMALES
Mexican steamed filled dumplings

TAMALES ARE one of my all-time favourite foods. This recipe was a staple item on the summer menu of my restaurant in California. Soft spiced dough steamed to perfection in dried corn husks and filled with roasted jalapeños, sweet potato and corn. What's not to like? It is a bit labour intensive to assemble the tamales, so give yourself plenty of time. That was the one drawback of being on the menu, they were very popular and often sold out.

The masa harina used for tamales is slightly more coarse; you can swap it for the masa used for tortillas and not notice too much of a difference. For a light fluffy tamale, it is helpful to have a stand mixer to incorporate the water and then the oil to the masa. This can also be done in a bowl by simply combining all of the ingredients for the dough, however, the finished tamale with be a bit denser. Traditionally lard is used, but I have found that a mild unflavoured coconut oil or vegan butter both work very well.

Serve with the salsa verde recipe found in this chapter. Can't find tomatillos for making salsa verde? Use another salsa or sauce recipe from this chapter. A tin of black beans can also be used instead of the sweetcorn.

FOR THE MASA DOUGH

200g masa harina for tamales (found in online Mexican shops)

200ml warm water

70g vegan butter or coconut oil, softened

1 tsp baking powder

½ tsp salt

½ tsp cumin

½ tsp cinnamon

FOR THE FILLING

1 large sweet potato, cut into 1 cm cubes

3 ears of sweetcorn or 150g frozen sweetcorn, thawed

3 jalapeños or green chillies, seeds removed and sliced into thin strips

1 tbsp olive oil

1 tsp cumin

½ tsp coriander

salt and pepper

4 spring onions, sliced on the diagonal

1 package cornhusks, soaked in hot water for at least 30 minutes and using a heavy plate to keep the husks submerged

salsa verde or other salsa to serve (see recipes)

In the bowl of a stand mixer, combine the masa harina, baking powder, salt, cumin and cinnamon. Turn the machine on low and slowly pour in the hot water. Once all the water is added, increase the speed and whip the masa for 5 minutes. Remove from the machine, cover with clingfilm and let stand for 30 minutes. This is to let the masa rehydrate. Return the masa to the stand mixer and mix at high speed for 5 minutes. Add the coconut oil or margarine 2-3 spoonfuls at a time. Once all the oil has been added, beat for another 5 minutes.

Preheat the oven to 200°C/Gas Mark 6. Place all the filling ingredients, except the spring onions, on a baking tray. Roast in the oven for 15-20 minutes stirring once or twice. When the sweet potatoes are tender, remove from the oven and stir in the spring onions.

After soaking and before using, rinse the cornhusks to remove any dirt or corn silk. Separate and stack the husks in a large bowl. To prevent the husks from drying out while working, cover the bowl with a clean, damp towel.

Prepare ties to secure the tamales by tearing one or two husks lengthwise into 1cm (¼ inch) thick strips. Each tamale will need two strips. Place a large cornhusk down on the counter; the sides of the husks should slightly roll into each other.

Spread about a golf ball size of masa dough on the smooth side of a cornhusk, leaving at least 5cm (2 inch) on each end. Place 2 tablespoons of filling in the middle of the dough. Roll the husk over until the sides of the dough touch. Continue rolling until the husk forms a cylinder. Twist at each end and secure by tying a knot with a strip.

Place the tamales in a steamer and bring to the boil. Steam for about 35 minutes or until firm to the touch, making sure if the tamales are stacked one or two high to rotate positions.

MOLE POBLANO

MOLE is the famous Mexican sauce made from dried chillies and chocolate, along with a host of other ingredients. Food is not always understood when taken out of the context of its origins. This rings especially true for mole; in Mexico mole is commonly served like gravy and poured over cooked meats. As I don't eat meat I use it over roasted squash, mushrooms or as a sauce for enchiladas or tamales. Maybe not the most traditional use, but it works. I have never taught this recipe in a class due to it being very time consuming and I hesitated including it in this book. Even if readers do not attempt to make it, it is a cultural reference for the complexity of this ancient cuisine.

My version is simplified due to availability of certain items, however it still contains 23 ingredients. The dried chillies all add different characteristics to the sauce. Anchos are mild, oxblood colour, wrinkly and add a sweetness with notes of bitter chocolate taste. Pasillas are medium hot, cocoa colour, rich and tangy tasting with notes of wood and herbs. Mulatos are chocolate brown, mild, rich with notes of dried fruit and liquorice. Despite the amount of chillies in this sauce, it is not overly hot as the seeds are removed. Keep some of the seeds back to add in if you would like it more spicy.

Allow plenty of time for this recipe. I have been making it for a long time and it still takes me the better part of 2 hours, but it is well worth the effort and as it makes a big batch, you will have plenty to freeze.

40g dried ancho chillies

30g dried pasilla chillies

40g dried mulato chillies

100ml sunflower, rapeseed or mild coconut oil for frying

40g sesame seeds

60g almonds

75g raisins

30g pumpkin seeds

2 corn tortillas, torn into strips

65g of stale baguette or similar bread, torn into pieces, use gluten free bread for gluten free

1 onion, finely chopped

4 cloves garlic, peeled and roughly chopped

1/2 ripe plantain or 1 banana

4 large tomatillos or 2 underripe plum tomatoes, roughly chopped

SPICES

10 peppercorns

2 cinnamon sticks, broken into several pieces

1/2 tsp anise seeds

8 whole cloves

1 tsp dried oregano, Mexican if possible

150g Mexican chocolate or dark bitter chocolate, broken into pieces

2 litres vegetable stock

2 tbsp of sugar, more to taste

salt to taste

With a pair of scissors, cut each chilli lengthwise to open then remove the seeds and cut out the stem. Heat 2 tbsp of the oil in a frying pan, using tongs, fry the chillies a few at a time to bring out the flavour, but careful not to burn. This will only take about 30 seconds on each side. Repeat until all the chilies are done, adding more oil when needed. Place the chillies in a bowl and cover with boiling water for 30 minutes to reconstitute. In the same frying pan heat 1 tablespoon of oil and fry the sesame seeds until golden and fragrant, this will happen quickly, do not burn. Remove sesame seeds from the pan and place on a plate lined with kitchen towel to absorb excess oil. Add another tablespoon of oil and repeat one at a time with the almonds, raisins and pumpkin seeds. Fry the bread and tortillas separately, adding more oil when needed until golden brown, about 2 minutes for the bread and 1 minute for the tortillas; remove from pan.

By this time the pan is very hot, so adjust heat when needed and mind the handle being hot. Heat another tablespoon of oil and fry the onion until golden, about 8-10 minutes. When the onion is golden, add the garlic and cook for another couple of minutes, being careful not to burn. Remove the onion and garlic from the pan and place in a bowl. Fry the plantain or banana in a bit of oil until brown, remove from the pan and add to the onions. Heat another tablespoon of oil and fry the tomatillos or tomatoes for about 5-8 minutes until soft; add to the same bowl as the onions. Turn off the heat and leave the pan to cool.

In a different frying pan, dry toast the peppercorns, cinnamon sticks, anise seeds and cloves (not the oregano) until fragrant, again be careful not to burn. Place in a spice grinder or use a pestle and mortar and grind until powder.

Strain the chillies and reserve the soaking liquid. Place the chillies and a bit of the soaking liquid in a blender and blend until smooth. Heat a large saucepan over a medium-high heat and add 3 tbsp of oil. Pour in the blended mixture and fry for 10-15 minutes until the colour starts to deepen and the mixture looks glossy. It will look a bit like tomato puree.

Blend all of the fried ingredients, the ground spices and oregano in a high speed blender along with a bit of the chilli soaking liquid and blend until smooth, adding more liquid if needed. Pass through a sieve if a smooth sauce is desired. Add to the cooking chillies. Cook for about 5 minutes.

Add chocolate and stock. Simmer for 1 hour, stirring regularly. Add sugar and salt. Taste and adjust the seasoning, adding more salt or sugar if needed. Reserved chilli seeds can be ground and added for extra heat. The final result should be a thick, rich dark red/brown sauce with a bit of heat and back notes of spices and chocolate.

PULLED JACKFRUIT TACOS

JACKFRUIT is by no means Mexican, however it is a great replacement for carnitas, pulled pork, which is very popular in Mexico.

SPICE BLEND
2 tsp ground cumin

2 tsp smoked paprika or chipotle paste, more to taste

1/2 tsp dried oregano

salt and pepper

pinch cinnamon

1 tbsp lime juice

FOR THE PULLED JACKFRUIT
1 tbsp rapeseed or sunflower oil

1 small onion, diced

2 garlic cloves, crushed

spice blend (above)

596g/20 oz tin of green Jackfruit in brine, drained and roughly chopped

2 tsp agave or maple syrup

100ml water

CHIPOTLE MAYO
50ml mayonnaise or vegan mayonnaise

1-2 tsp chipotle paste, to taste

squeeze of lime juice

GARNISHES
taco shells, soft corn tortillas or little gem lettuce leaves

radish slices

shredded cabbage

fresh coriander

Place a frying pan on medium heat. Add the oil and let warm; add the onion with a pinch of salt and cook for 3-5 minutes. Add garlic and the spice blend and cook for 2 minutes stirring regularly.

To prep the jackfruit, slice the core from the fibrous bit and finely chop the core. Slice the fibrous bit, but do not chop too much.

Add the jackfruit, agave syrup and water, stir well to combine. Cover and cook for 5-10 minutes or until half the liquid is absorbed. Uncover and start to break up the jackfruit using the back of a wooden spoon. It will be ready when the liquid is dissolved and the jackfruit darkens and starts to look shredded. Turn down the heat and cook a bit longer until it starts to stick to the pan. Do not burn, just cook down a bit longer, adding a splash of water if needed. Taste and adjust the seasoning if needed.

To make the chipotle mayo, combine the mayonnaise, chipotle paste and lime juice. Taste and add more lime, mayo or chipotle if desired.

Place the jackfruit on heated soft tacos or taco shells and garnish with radish, cabbage, coriander and chipotle mayo.

RICE AND BEANS are the staple of many Mexican households. Economical, nutritious, quick and easy, but also full of flavour and very satisfying. Think about it, if you could only afford rice and beans plus a few spices you would make it as delicious as possible. Knowing that you may eat it day in and day out.

- 1 small onion, very finely chopped
- 400g fresh and cored tomatoes or tinned chopped
- 3 garlic cloves
- 1 tbsp rapeseed oil
- 1 tsp cumin seeds
- 1 tsp coriander seeds
- 250g white long grain rice
- 450ml hot water
- pinch of salt
- fresh lime juice, to taste
- fresh coriander, finely chopped

Blend the onion, tomatoes and garlic using a hand blender or food processor. Rinse the rice under cold water to remove starches and shake vigorously to drain the excess water. Heat the oil in a pan. Add the cumin and coriander seeds and fry for 2-3 minutes, until fragrant. Add the rice and cook for a few more minutes. Add the blended tomato mixture and stir well.

Pour in the hot water and add the pinch of salt. Bring to a boil then reduce the heat to a simmer and cover. Cook for 15 minutes or until the water is absorbed and the rice is tender. Check towards the end; if the rice looks dry add a little more water. Leave to sit for 5 minutes then fluff with a fork. Add lime juice to taste and garnish with fresh coriander.

REFRIED BEANS

BEANS are very special in Mexico and deliver taste, texture, colour and nutritional value. Long simmered black beans are found everywhere and are delicious, but take a couple of days to make. This is a homemade version of the refried pinto beans that you can purchase in a tin here in the UK.

Espazote is a culinary herb used in Mexico for flavour and to release gases from the beans. It's available online or in Mexican shops in the UK, but it's not essential. It is added to help with digestion.

250g dry pinto beans (need soaking overnight)

2 sprigs or 1 tsp espazote (optional)

2 tbsp sunflower oil

1 small onion, finely chopped

3-4 garlic cloves, finely chopped

1 tsp ground cumin

salt to taste

Soak the beans overnight, drain and rinse. Place the beans in a pot and cover with water, about 5cm (2 inch) above the beans, and add the espazote if using. Cook until tender; this usually takes about 1 hour. Do not drain.

Heat the frying pan on a medium heat, allowing the oil to warm up. Add the onion and sauté for 3-4 minutes. Add the garlic and cumin and stir. Cook for about a minute. Using a slotted spoon, add about two spoonfuls of beans to the onion mixture and mash with the back of the spoon or a mashing utensil. If the mixture seems thick, add a tablespoon of the cooking liquid from the beans. Continue to add beans and mash them together, incorporating liquid as necessary. Cook until warm throughout. Add salt to taste.

MEXICAN WEDDING CAKES

MEXICAN WEDDING CAKES are actually not cakes but biscuits and are another example of culinary influence from Spain. These little cookies are traditionally served at weddings. In Mexico, they are referred to as biscochitos. The recipe has many variations and names around the world and is basically a shortbread with added nuts covered in icing sugar. What is not to like!

65g toasted nuts - almonds, pecans or walnuts

260g plain flour or gluten free plain flour

225g butter, at room temperature, and a little more for greasing

30g icing sugar

pinch of salt

FOR THE TOPPING
100g icing sugar, sifted

FOR A VEGAN VERSION
Use coconut oil or good quality vegan margarine instead of butter

Preheat the oven to 180°C/Gas Mark 4. Toast the nuts by placing them on a baking tray and baking for about 8 minutes or until lightly brown and fragrant. Leave to cool. Once the nuts have cooled completely place them, along with 2 tablespoons of the flour into your food processor and process until they are finely ground. Set aside.

In the food processor, cream together the butter and icing sugar. Add the remaining flour and a pinch of salt. Pulse until combined. Stir in the nuts. Cover and refrigerate the dough for about an hour or until firm.

Form the chilled dough into 2.5cm (1 inch) balls with your hands or a scoop and place them 5cm (2 inch) apart on greased baking trays. Bake for 12-15 minutes or until the edges of the cookies start to brown. Remove from the oven and place on a wire rack to cool.

Place some icing sugar in a bowl and roll the slightly cooled cookies in the sugar to coat.

CHURROS

THIS RECIPE FOR CHURROS came about from one of my collaborations. It was one of my Meat Free Mondays hosted by Asparagasm at The Royal Oak in Tetbury. Asparagasm is a gluten free, vegan and refined sugar free brand started originally in London by the bodacious Kate Lewis. Kate and I have collaborated over the years on various events and she is truly a gem to work with. Her creativity and optimism is contagious. Thank you Kate, for everything, long may our collaborations continue. The original recipe uses gluten free flour and coconut sugar; if that is not necessary for you or you would prefer to use wheat flour and cane sugar, plain white flour and golden sugar can be swapped. Churros are interesting because they are made like a choux pastry and then deep fried like a doughnut, yum!

125g gluten free plain flour, plain flour from wheat works fine as well

30g coconut sugar or golden sugar

1/2 tsp baking powder

pinch of sea salt

300ml water

1 tsp vanilla paste

2tbsp coconut oil

500ml rapeseed or sunflower oil for frying

SUGAR COATING

50g coconut sugar or caster sugar

2 tsp ground cinnamon

pinch sea salt

In a bowl, whisk together flour, sugar and a pinch of salt. In a small saucepan, combine the water, vanilla paste and coconut oil. Bring to a boil, then reduce the heat to a simmer. Quickly add all the flour mixture and stir until the dough comes away from the sides of the pan, 1 to 2 minutes. Remove from the heat and transfer to a large bowl. Set aside to cool.

In a large saucepan over a medium heat, heat the oil to 190°C. Meanwhile, in a large bowl, whisk together coconut sugar, cinnamon and salt. Set aside.

Fill a piping bag with dough and working in batches of 2 or 3, squeeze strips of dough 2-3 inches/5-7.5 cm long and about 1/2inch/1 cm in diameter into hot oil. Cook for 6 to 7 minutes, or until churros are crisp and golden brown.

Using a slotted spoon, transfer to a plate lined with kitchen towel to drain for a minute and then into the bowl with cinnamon sugar. Toss to coat well. Transfer to a serving plate. Repeat with remaining batter. Serve immediately.

CHOCOLATE SAUCE

400ml tin of coconut milk

100g agave syrup or coconut sugar

40g cocoa powder

2 tbsp coconut oil

1/2 tsp vanilla, optional

Whisk the coconut milk, agave syrup or coconut sugar and cocoa powder until very well combined. Pour into a saucepan and bring to a gently simmer. Allow to simmer lightly, stirring very frequently for 10 minutes. Remove from heat and add the vanilla extract and coconut oil. Stir until totally blended. Allow to cool at room temperature.

MIDDLE EASTERN MEZZE

A MEZZE is a meal or a course consisting of a variety of small dishes served at once, similar to tapas in Spain or an Indian thali. In my humble opinion, this is one of the best ways to share a meal. A selection of dips, vegetable dishes, maybe something wrapped in flakey filo, and crunchy herb filled falafels. I usually add some fresh salad leaves and never forget the gorgeous flatbread to mop it all up with.

My Middle Eastern Mezze class is always popular in the summer months as the ingredients are best when the weather's warmer. These dishes are great served all together but can also be cherry picked to accompany a picnic, barbeque or part of a more formal sit down meal.

Throughout the chapter, you'll find ingredients like pomegranate molasses, ras el hanout, sumac and za'atar. Don't be put off if you don't have these ingredients to hand, or don't know how to use them - you'll find many of them in your local supermarket. Each of the recipes will explain what they are and how to use them. After tasting what they bring to a meal you'll always want them in your cupboard.

RAS EL HANOUT ROASTED VEGETABLES & HALOUMI *with pomegranate molasses*

RAS EL HANOUT and pomegranate molasses are not part of everyone's cupboard staples, but once you taste the fragrant flavours you'll find many uses for both.

Ras el hanout is a North African spice blend that is similar to garam masala in Indian cooking. The name is Arabic for 'head of the shop' (similar to the English expression 'top-shelf') and implies a mixture of the best spices the seller has to offer. Commonly used ingredients include cardamom, cumin, clove, cinnamon, nutmeg, mace, allspice, ginger, chilli peppers, coriander seed, peppercorns, sweet and hot paprika, fenugreek, and turmeric.

Pomegranate molasses is pomegranate juice that has been reduced, with or without sugar, to a thick, intensely flavoured syrup. Although it's a syrup, it's not overly sweet, it has a depth of flavour and is tangy. It can also be used in salad dressings or as a glaze, or added to dips like hummus, as well as to flavour cold drinks.

Serve as part of a mezze or with warm flat bread and a green salad.

FOR THE ROASTED VEGETABLES:

1 aubergine, cut into 2.5cm (1 inch) pieces

1 red pepper, cut into 2.5cm (1 inch) pieces

1 orange/yellow pepper, cut into 2.5cm (1 inch) pieces

1 courgette, cut into 2.5cm (1 inch) pieces

1 large red onion, cut into eight wedges, leaving a little bit of the roots attached

200g cherry tomatoes, left whole

2 tbsp olive oil

salt and pepper

1 tbsp ras el hanout

fresh flat leafed parsley, finely chopped

lemon juice

FOR THE HALOUMI WITH POMEGRANATE MOLASSES:

1 tbsp olive oil

1 packet haloumi, about 300 grams, in 1cm slices

2 tbsp pomegranate molasses

3 mint sprigs, leaves only

FOR A VEGAN VERSION

Replace the haloumi with firm tofu.

For the roasted vegetables: place all the prepared vegetables in a bowl. Add the oil, salt and pepper and ras el hanout and toss well to coat. Spread the vegetables between two baking trays and roast them for 45 minutes to an hour, turning every 10-15 minutes. The vegetables are done when they are tender and starting to colour. Arrange on a serving plate and garnish with parsley and lemon juice.

For the Haloumi: add the olive oil to a large frying pan over medium-high heat. Heat for 1 minute then add the haloumi slices. Cook for 2 minutes on each side until golden brown. Arrange the cheese around the roasted vegetables. Drizzle the pomegranate molasses over the cheese, and sprinkle with mint leaves.

TZATZIKI

A GREAT MEZZE should consist of at least one finger licking dip. Here are a few traditional ones that are always a hit.

½ cucumber, grated

6-8 fresh mint springs, leaves only, finely chopped

1 small garlic clove, finely chopped or grated

½ tsp dried dill or 2 tsp fresh dill, finely chopped

500ml thick Greek yoghurt

salt and pepper

FOR A VEGAN VERSION
Use a thick non-dairy yoghurt such as coconut

Coarsely grate the cucumber. Using your hands or muslin, squeeze out the excess juice into the sink. Place all the ingredients in a bowl and combine. Taste and adjust the seasoning.

BABA GHANOUSH

2 large or 3 medium aubergines

3 tbsp olive oil

1 small garlic clove, finely chopped or grated

juice of ½ lemon

3 fresh parsley sprigs, roughly chopped

salt and pepper

Preheat the oven to 220°C/Gas Mark 7.

Prick the aubergine with a fork a couple of times to prevent explosion. Place on a baking sheet and into the hot oven. Roast for 45-60 minutes or until the aubergines have collapsed, turning every 15 minutes. This can also be done on the barbeque, under the grill or over an open fire.

Remove the aubergines from the oven and allow to cool for a few minutes. When cool enough to handle, scoop the aubergine flesh out of the charred skins and place into a sieve to drain for a bit.

Put the aubergine into a bowl and add the remaining ingredients; combine with a fork, gently breaking up the flesh as you go.

SERVES 8

HUMMUS

HUMMUS made with dried chickpeas that are soaked and then cooked is a bit more time consuming, but so worth the effort. To do this, simply use 100g dried chickpeas per 400g tin, so this recipe would need 200g.

2 x 400g tinned chickpeas (reserve the liquid and a few chickpeas for decoration) or 200g dry, see above

3 tbsp lemon juice, freshly squeezed, more to taste

2 garlic cloves, finely chopped, more to taste

½ tsp salt, more to taste

1 tbsp tahini, more to taste

5 tbsp extra virgin olive oil

paprika or sumac to garnish

Put the chickpeas in a bowl and cover with twice the volume of cold water. Stir in 1 teaspoon of bicarbonate of soda and leave to soak for 24 hours. Drain the chickpeas, rinse well and place in a saucepan. Cover with cold water and add ½ teaspoon of bicarb. The bicarb is to help soften the skin, make the chickpeas easier to digest and reduce the cooking time, but is not necessary and can be omitted. Bring to the boil, then turn down the heat and simmer gently until they're tender – they need to be easy to mush, and almost falling apart, which will take between 1 and 3 hours depending on your chickpeas. Add more hot water if they seem to be boiling dry. Remember to reserve some of the cooking water when draining. Reserve the liquid when draining the chickpeas, then rinse. Combine the chickpeas (reserving a few), lemon juice, garlic, salt, tahini, and about 100ml of reserved chickpea water in a food processor, and whiz to a creamy purée.

Add more lemon juice, tahini, garlic or salt to taste. Turn out into a bowl, and smooth with the back of a spoon. Drizzle with the extra virgin olive oil and scatter with the reserved chickpeas. Sprinkle with paprika or sumac and serve.

ZA'ATAR FLATBREAD

FLATBREADS play an important role in a mezze, helping you mop it all up! This recipe is a basic pitta recipe that I have added a za'atar and olive oil topping to. Top tips when baking any yeasted bread product: use strong flour and do not mix the salt with the yeast until you are ready to add the water. Salt kills yeast.

10g dried yeast

300ml tepid water

500g strong white bread flour

1 tsp salt

2 tbsp olive oil

FOR THE TOPPING
4 heaped tbsp za'atar (shop bought or homemade, see below)

50ml olive oil

ZA'ATAR SPICE BLEND
2 tbsp sesame seeds

4 tbsp ground sumac

3 tbsp dried thyme

2 tbsp dried oregano

1 tsp salt

Measure the flour in a large bowl, tip the measured salt to one side and the measured yeast to the other. Make a well in the middle of the flour and add all the water. Form a dough and bring out onto the counter. Spread the dough out into a rectangle and add the olive oil. Knead until smooth and firm, about 10 minutes.

To make the za'atar, gently toast the sesame seeds in a dry frying pan until popping and fragrant. Remove from pan and let cool. In a bowl mix together sesame seeds, sumac, thyme, oregano and salt. If you would like a finer blend, the mixture can be put through a spice grinder.

Form the dough into a ball and place it in a lightly oiled bowl. Cover the bowl with clingfilm and leave to rise in a warm, draught-free place for about 1 hour until it doubles in size.

Preheat the oven to 220°C/Gas Mark 7. Divide the dough into eight balls. Place the balls on a lightly oiled baking sheet, cover with a damp cloth or oiled clingfilm, and allow to stand for about 15 minutes.

Meanwhile, combine the za'atar topping ingredients in a small bowl. Note you will not need all of the za'atar spice blend, the rest will store happily in a jar for about 6 months.

Lightly flour a surface and flatten each ball of dough and roll it into a circle 0.3cm (⅛ inch) thick and about 18-20cm (7-8 inch) in diameter. Alternatively, roll out long oval shaped pittas. Press each circle with your fingertips to make little indentations for the topping to settle in. Spread 1 heaped tablespoon of za'atar topping over each round, leaving a 1.25cm (½ inch) border around the edges.

Bake for about 6-8 minutes or until lightly browned and crisp. You may need to do several batches depending on the size of your oven. Serve warm right away, keep warm in folded tea towels or cool on racks.

PITTA BREADS

TO MAKE PITTA BREADS, simply use the same dough and omit the topping.

Preheat the oven to the hottest setting and place a baking tray or pizza stone in the oven. Divide the dough by eight for large pitta or twelve for smaller and roll out into flat, but even ovals. Carefully remove the tray from the oven and place the rolled dough on the hot tray. If using a stone, place the rolled dough in the oven, directly on the stone. You may have to do this in batches. Bake for 2-4 minutes depending on the size of the pitta until puffed and turning slightly golden in a spot or two, but generally still pale. Be careful not to over bake; pitta are soft and do not have too much colour. Remove from the oven and repeat if needed.

FATTOUSH

THIS SALAD is a great way to use up old pittas and create an unforgettable summer salad. Sumac is a reddish-purplish powder made from dried and crushed fruits produced by one of the varieties of the sumac plant. It's used in salads, to sprinkle on hummus and other mezze dishes or rice, adding a wonderful tart, lemony flavour. In the spring, I often make a pea, radish and mint salad liberally sprinkled with sumac.

2 large pitta breads, use gluten free pitta for gluten free

olive oil

½ cucumber, sliced

500g ripe cherry tomatoes, halved

1 red pepper, chopped

4 spring onions, thinly sliced or 2 shallots

3 tbsp flat leaf parsley, roughly chopped

3 tbsp fresh mint leaves, roughly chopped

sumac to sprinkle

salt and pepper to taste

crunchy lettuce leaves, like cos or romaine to serve

FOR THE DRESSING

3 tbsp olive oil

2 tbsp lemon juice

1 small garlic clove, finely chopped

1 tbsp sumac, plus a little for garnish

Preheat the oven to 200°C/Gas Mark 6.

Brush the pitta with olive oil, then cut into 6-8 strips and spread on a baking tray so they are not too crowded; use a second baking tray if necessary. Drizzle with olive oil and bake for 10-15 minutes or until crispy, turning over halfway. Cool and then crumble.

Make the dressing by combining all the ingredients in a big bowl then add the prepared vegetables, chopped herbs and toasted pitta. Taste and adjust the seasoning. If time allows, leave to marinate for about 30 minutes. Arrange a variety of torn lettuce leaves on a serving dish and top with the salad. Sprinkle with sumac and enjoy.

SERVES 6

GREEK GREEN BEANS *with tomatoes*

MY MOM grew green beans (any variety of French beans) every summer and I was made to pick them on a regular basis. Back then I hated it as I would have much rather been playing with my friends. Now, I have my own allotment and always grow green beans. This recipe is a great way to use up the summer gluts and can be served as a side dish or as part of a mezze.

olive oil

1 large onion, finely chopped

3 medium tomatoes,
sliced into eights

500g French beans,
topped and tailed

1 tsp dried oregano or
1 tbsp fresh, finely chopped

salt and pepper

juice of 1 lemon

fresh parsley

Heat 2-3 tablespoons of olive oil in a large frying pan. Add the onion and cook until turning translucent. Add the chopped tomatoes and simmer for 5 minutes.

Add the French beans and oregano and season with salt and pepper. Cover and simmer until the beans are tender, about 8-10 minutes. Remove from the heat and finish with freshly squeezed lemon juice. Garnish with fresh parsley.

SERVES 4-6

MARINATED OLIVES

FRESH MARINATED OLIVES can be quite expensive and can be easily made at home. This recipe is herby and lemony however many combinations can be made, just experiment. Serve with flatbreads or pittas and hummus.

350g olives of your choice, drained weight

2 tbsp fresh thyme, finely chopped

1 small sprig fresh rosemary, torn into a few pieces

zest and juice of 1 lemon

4 garlic cloves, finely chopped or grated

3 tbsp olive oil

freshly ground pepper to taste

Combine the olives, thyme, rosemary, lemon zest, lemon juice, garlic, oil and pepper in a bowl and mix well. Cover and leave to marinate for at least 2 hours and up to 2 days before eating. Stir several times while marinating.

FALAFELS

THERE ARE so many falafel recipes out there it's a bit overwhelming. I've tried many over the years only to be disappointed by the mushy texture. Most recipes call for tinned chickpeas but this recipe uses dried chickpeas that are soaked overnight in bicarbonate of soda, then drained and rinsed, but not cooked - the texture is amazing. The flavour is herby and actually they are really quite easy to make. The cooked balls freeze well too, so you may as well make a double batch! Serve with pitta, tzatziki, hummus, salad and whatever else you like, but I guarantee you will eat one of the falafels before they get to the table!

250g dry chickpeas, soaked overnight with ½ tsp bicarbonate of soda

4-6 garlic cloves, peeled

1 small onion, peeled and roughly chopped

30g flat leaf parsley, large stems removed and roughly chopped

30g fresh coriander leaves, large stems removed and roughly chopped

10g fresh dill, large stems removed and roughly chopped

2 tsp ground cumin

2 tsp ground coriander

½ tsp paprika or chilli powder

1 tsp salt

1 tsp baking powder

rapeseed or sunflower oil for deep frying

Drain and rinse the chickpeas. Combine the chickpeas with the garlic, onion, parsley and coriander leaves. Blitz in a food processor until roughly chopped, but not pulverized. The mixture should not be a puree, but should retain texture. Add the cumin, coriander, paprika, salt and baking powder. Pulse in the food processor until the dough starts to form a ball. Leave to rest in the fridge for 2-3 hours.

Heat a deep fat fryer or half fill a large heavy-based saucepan or wok with rapeseed or sunflower oil to about 180°C. Form the falafel mixture into small walnut sized portions using a scoop or your hands. When the oil is hot, drop in a falafel; if it starts to fall apart the oil may not be hot enough or may be too hot. Check the temperature. Cook about 5 or 6 at a time but do not overload the pan/fryer. Turn after about 3 minutes, then when golden on both sides remove and drain on kitchen towels. Slice one in half to make sure it is cooked all the way through, if not, place back in oil and cook for a few more minutes.

The falafels can also be brushed with oil and baked at 200°C for 20 minutes, turning once or pan-fried with less oil, however, they are the most delicious when deep fried.

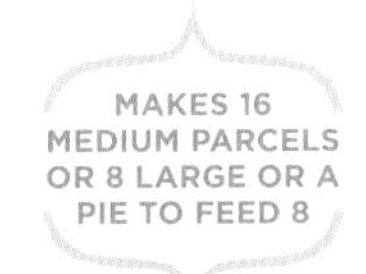

SPANAKOPITA

FOR ME, as a young university student and very new to being vegetarian, spanakopita was love at first bite. It has been a long relationship and lasted throughout the years, altered for when I was vegan and enhanced when I started growing my own herbs. I'm still very much head over heels for this dish, but nothing quite matches my first experience at a Greek dinner in Columbia, South Carolina. Here are instructions for both individual triangles and one big pie.

3 tbsp pine nuts or cashews

olive oil, for frying onions and brushing filo

2 medium onions, finely chopped

750g frozen spinach, thawed and squeezed to remove excess water

30g flat leaf parsley, finely chopped

20g fresh dill, finely chopped or 1 tbsp dried

juice of 1 lemon

¼ tsp fresh grated nutmeg, more to taste

200g feta cheese

1 free-range egg, beaten

75g melted butter for brushing

2 tbsp olive oil

salt and freshly ground black pepper

ready made filo pastry sheets

mixed herbs

FOR A VEGAN VERSION
Omit the egg and substitute the feta for firm tofu, adding 2 tablespoons olive oil and a bit more lemon juice, and use olive oil for brushing the filo sheets

Toast the pine nuts or cashews in a dry frying pan until golden, being careful not to burn. Set aside. Using the same pan, gently sauté the onion in olive oil until golden.

Meanwhile, for the filling, in a large bowl, combine the nuts with the spinach, parsley, dill, lemon, and nutmeg. Add the cooked onion to the spinach mix. Now add the feta and mix well. Season with salt and pepper, taste and adjust the seasoning. When happy with the seasoning, mix in the beaten egg.

Lay the stack of filo sheets on a work surface. Remove one sheet and place it lengthways in front of you. Keep the remaining sheets covered with a damp towel. Brush the sheet with melted butter and olive oil. Place a second sheet of filo on top, brush it with the melted butter. Add 1 more sheet in the same manner.

Cut the stack of filo sheets lengthwise into 4 for smaller parcels or 2 for larger parcels. Starting at the bottom right corner, place a heaped dessert spoonful of filling, leaving a triangle of filo on the left side. Use two spoonfuls for larger parcels. Fold the end of the filo diagonally over the filling, enclosing the filling completely and creating a 10cm (4 inch) triangle; the bottom edge of the strip should now be even with the left side of the strip.

Next, fold the bottom of the triangle up, so that it meets the straight edge evenly. Now fold again on the diagonal, so that the left edge is even with the right side. Repeat this folding pattern, alternating the direction with each fold, until you reach the end of the strip. Repeat with the remaining strip, to make another triangle. Place the triangles on the prepared baking sheet. Continue until filo or filling runs out!

When all the triangles are assembled, brush with olive oil and sprinkle with mixed herbs. Place in a hot oven and bake for 25-30 minutes or until puffy and golden brown. If you are freezing or reheating another time, only par bake until there is a bit of colour just starting to show, about 10-15 minutes.

TO MAKE ONE LARGE DISH OF SPANAKOPITA:
Grease a shallow baking dish with oil and line with six of the filo sheets, placing one on top of the other and brushing each sheet separately. Put the filling over the pastry and spread evenly. Cover with the remaining filo, brushing each sheet with oil as you go. Brush the top with oil and, with the point of a sharp knife, cut the crust into square pieces which will make it easier to cut once cooked. Bake for 40 minutes or until golden brown. Remove and leave to let sit for 10 minutes before serving.

SERVES 12

BAKLAVA

FLAKEY FILO, meaty nuts and sticky syrup, what more could you ask for? The more you make this dish, the better you get at it. I was recipe testing for this book and brought some of the leftovers to a barbeque. At first it was overlooked and I heard someone say that they didn't care for it. Half an hour later, the tray was empty and said person was liking his fingers after scoffing his third piece. Enough said.

The secret to avoiding soggy baklava: make the syrup first and leave it to cool, then pour over the baklava when it's removed from the oven. Alternatively let the baklava cool and pour the hot syrup over. Do not combine when both are hot.

18 sheets of ready-made filo pastry

100g butter, plus extra for greasing

300g mixed pistachios and walnuts, roughly chopped

2 tbsp sugar

1 tsp ground cinnamon

FOR THE SYRUP

200g granulated sugar

150ml water

1 tbsp lemon juice

zest of one orange

FOR A VEGAN VERSION

Use a light flavoured oil such as light olive oil or coconut for brushing

VE

Preheat the oven to 180°C/Gas Mark 5 and grease a 17 x 28cm (11 x 7 inch) or similar baking tray with butter. Melt the butter in a saucepan over a low heat. Place the filo on the baking tray, cutting it to fit if need be. Lay 10 sheets of filo pastry, one at a time, into the tray, brushing each sheet with the melted butter before adding the next.

In a bowl, mix together the nuts, sugar and cinnamon and spread the mixture over the pastry in the tray. Layer up the remaining sheets on top of the nut mixture, brushing each sheet with butter, as before. Using a sharp knife, cut a criss-cross pattern through the top layers of the pastry; this will make it easier to cut.

Place the baklava in the preheated oven for approximately 20 minutes, then decrease the oven temperature to 150°C and cook for an additional 30-40 minutes, or until the pastry is slightly puffed and golden on top. Do not allow the top to burn; cover with kitchen foil if it turns too quickly.

Remove the baklava from the oven and allow to cool slightly. Pour the syrup into the slits in the baklava and leave to cool completely. Cut into small diamond-shaped pieces and serve.

SERVES 6

ROASTED PLUMS *with honey and thyme*

IMAGINE hillsides full of wild thyme, local honey and fresh summer plums. This pudding is a gorgeous blend of fragrant herbs, tart plums and sweet syrup. It's simple to make, but will impress at any dinner party or get together.

50g brown sugar

50g honey

50g butter

25g fresh thyme sprigs, reserve some to garnish; the flowers make a lovely garnish too

4 cardamom pods, smashed

800g ripe but firm medium-large plums, halved and stone removed

Greek yoghurt

FOR A VEGAN VERSION

Substitute the butter with vegan margarine or coconut oil, use vegan yoghurt and replace the honey with agave syrup

Preheat the oven to 200°C/Gas Mark 6. Combine the brown sugar, honey, butter, thyme and cardamom in a bowl and stir well. Pour onto a baking tray and turn all the plums so they are cut side down. Place in the oven and and bake for 5 minutes.

Remove the tray from the oven and flip the plums over so the cut side is up. Baste the plums with the sauce. Return the tray to the oven and bake for another 5 minutes, smaller or very ripe plums may require less time. If the sauce is very thin, it can be reduced in a saucepan to reach desired consistency.

Serve the plums with remaining syrup, Greek yoghurt and garnish with the additional thyme sprigs or flowers.

MOROCCAN NIGHTS

MOROCCO is a diverse country of vibrant cities, long coastlines, rugged interior mountains and large deserts. As with many countries the food has been influenced by years of interaction and exchange from other places. The cuisine has traces of Spanish, French, Portuguese and Berber, but still manages to maintain a unique identity. Moroccan recipes have a way of combining strong flavours and fresh ingredients in a way that ends in a perfectly balanced smooth and subtle taste.

Street food is a long standing tradition and is best experienced by a visit to the Djemaa el Fna square in Marrakech. The square is almost empty by day, bar the odd fruit, nut and orange juice vendor or snake charmer. But as the sun approaches its initial decent out come the vendors with their matching stalls, ready to set up and begin cooking a feast not just for visitors, but locals as well. The smells are enticing, the street performers captivating and the swindlers quick to catch the naive tourist. It's intense and should be experienced by anyone visiting the city, at least once. We ate there most nights, seeking out the stalls in the centre of the market where we saw the locals queuing for their favorites.

ORANGE & DATE SALAD *with preserved lemons and sumac*

MOROCCAN MEALS often include a sweet salad to counter the spicy dishes. This fruit salad is beautiful and goes very well with a spread of tagine, couscous and flatbreads. Blood oranges are fabulous to use when in season as they provide gorgeous colour and fantastic flavour.

Orange blossom water can be found in most supermarkets these days or in world food shops. It is delicious added to brownies, cakes, cocktails, sprinkled over fruit salad or whisked into salad dressings. It can even be used in your iron for a gentle fragrance, a few drops added to a bowl of water and placed by a radiator or as a slightly astringent facial toner.

3-4 oranges

150g dried dates

2-3 tbsp orange blossom water

½ a preserved lemon (optional)

1 tsp sumac

Cut the top and bottom off each orange so the flesh is visible, maybe 1.25cm (½ inch) depending on the thickness of the peel. Next, to remove the peel, cut from top to bottom curving the knife to the shape of the orange. Repeat all the way around. Place the oranges on a plate to catch the juice and finely slice them into circles. Remove and discard the seeds then put the slices in a shallow bowl with the juice.

Slice the dates lengthways into quarters and scatter over the oranges. Pour the orange blossom water over the oranges and dates. Gently toss using your hands to combine. Cover the bowl and leave for 15 minutes so the flavours mingle and the dates soften.

Cut the preserved lemon in half, remove all the flesh, seeds and pith and finely slice or chop the peel. Arrange the oranges and dates on a plate in a decorative manner. Scatter the preserved lemon and sumac over the oranges and dates.

MOROCCAN STUFFED FLATBREAD

THESE FLATBREADS are simple to make and absolutely delicious. Don't be worried if the filling pokes through the dough it will be fine in the end. The filling possibilities are infinite - a variety of fresh herbs, spices and tastes can be added to create your own favourite.

FOR THE DOUGH
½ tsp dried yeast

125ml slightly warm water

250g plain flour

½ tsp salt

FOR THE FILLING
4-6 spring onions, finely chopped

large handful of flat leaf parsley, finely chopped

60g butter, softened

2 tsp paprika

1 tsp ground cumin

pinch of salt

oil for rolling and cooking

ALTERNATIVE FILLING
5cm (2 inch) fresh ginger, peeled and finely chopped or grated

4 garlic cloves, peeled and finely chopped

1 green chilli, finely chopped

50g desiccated coconut

60g butter, softened

2 tsp paprika

FOR A VEGAN VERSION
Use good quality vegan butter or coconut oil

Measure the flour in a large bowl, tip the measured salt to one side and the measured yeast to the other. Make a well in the middle of the flour and add all the water. Form a dough and bring out onto the counter. Knead the dough briefly on a lightly oiled work surface, then cover with an inverted bowl and allow to rest for 15 minutes. The dough will be quite firm and dry; this is fine as it will change as it rests.

For the filling, combine the onion, parsley, butter, spices and salt in a bowl and mix well.

Smear your work surface and hands with a little oil and divide the dough into 4 equal portions. Shape each into a ball. Working 1 ball at a time, flatten the dough with a rolling pin into a rectangle about half the size of an A4 piece of paper. If the dough is elastic and wants to spring back, let it rest for a few moments, then try again. The dough should be as thin as you can make it without tearing.

With the dough in 'portrait' orientation, spread a quarter of the filling over the centre of the dough. Fold the bottom to the middle, then the top to the middle, like a letter. Then fold one side over the middle and one side under to create a 7.5cm (3 inch) square. Repeat with the other three balls.

Preheat a frying pan to a medium heat and add some oil to lightly grease it. Cook the flattened squares on both sides until golden brown, about 2-3 minutes per side. Turn the heat down if the flatbreads are browning too quickly to ensure that the inside dough is cooked as well. Slice into halves or quarters to expose the filling. Serve hot or warm.

HARISSA

HARISSA is a condiment made of roasted red peppers, spices and chilli. It's commonly served alongside meals to add a spicy element to dishes. It's also used as a rub in recipes and for flavouring couscous. It can be found in most supermarkets, however making your own has multiple benefits. You can control the heat, what spices are added, and the taste is far better. It keeps in the fridge for 3-4 days and also freezes well. I always make a double or triple batch and freeze some for quick, tasty meals when I'm pushed for time.

2 fresh red chillies, seeded and chopped (depending on hotness!) or 3 dried

1 small red pepper

½ tsp each coriander seeds, cumin seeds and caraway seeds

1 tbsp olive oil

1 red onion, peeled and chopped

3 garlic cloves, peeled and chopped

2 tbsp tomato puree

2 tbsp lemon juice

½ tsp coarse sea salt

chilli powder to taste, optional

If using dried chillies, deseed and soak in 150ml of hot water for 10 minutes then drain and discard the water.

Place the red pepper under a very hot grill for 15-20 minutes or until the skin is blackened, or place directly on a gas burner. Transfer to a bowl, cover with a plate or clingfilm and set aside. Once the pepper is cool, peel off and discard the skin.

Place a dry frying pan on a medium heat and toast the coriander, cumin and caraway seeds for two minutes or until fragrant. Transfer to a mortar and pestle or spice grinder and grind to a powder.

Heat the oil in a frying pan and fry the onion and garlic over a medium heat until dark and smoky - around 6-8 minutes. Blend with a hand blender or in a food processor with the rest of the ingredients, including the now peeled pepper and fresh or soaked chillies. This can also be done with a mortar and pestle.

Taste and adjust the seasoning. Add chilli powder to taste.

CHICKPEAS & SPINACH *with chermoula*

CHICKPEAS AND SPINACH are two of the most universally liked ingredients. Paired together with chermoula, a marinade made from garlic, herbs and lemon, then finished with creamy yoghurt, this dish delivers. To ensure the yoghurt does not curdle, before stirring it in, remove the dish from the heat and leave to cool for a minute. If the yoghurt does curdle, don't worry it's fine to eat.

Frozen spinach also works great in this recipe. I tend to keep it on hand so I can just chuck it into recipes when I feel like I need a few more greens in my life. Use the same amount of fresh as frozen, thaw first and then squeeze out a bit of the excess water.

TO MAKE THE CHERMOULA
2-3 garlic cloves

½ tsp paprika

½ tsp ground cumin

1 tbsp harissa, shop bought or homemade (see recipe)

3 tbsp fresh flat leaf parsley, roughly chopped

3 tbsp fresh coriander, roughly chopped

2 tbsp lemon juice

3 tbsp olive oil

½ preserved lemon, roughly chopped

¼ tsp salt

FOR THE CHICKPEAS & SPINACH
1 tbsp olive oil

1 tbsp butter

2 garlic cloves, finely chopped

2 x 400g tin chickpeas, drained and rinsed

100ml water

200g baby spinach or roughly chopped larger spinach or chard

4 tbsp Greek yoghurt

FOR A VEGAN VERSION
Use vegan butter and vegan yoghurt

To make the chermoula, place all the chermoula ingredients into a blender and blend until smooth. Set aside.

Heat a large frying pan or saucepan with a lid over a medium heat. Add the oil and butter and sauté the garlic for about 30 seconds, being careful not to burn. Add the chermoula, chickpeas and 100ml of water, simmer for 5 minutes.

Stir in the spinach and cover with a lid. Cook until the spinach has just wilted. Remove from the heat, leave to cool a minute then stir in the yoghurt and season with salt and pepper to taste.

WINTER SQUASH *and* LENTIL TAGINE

THE WORD TAGINE refers to the cooking vessel, not the dish. It's an earthenware pot consisting of two parts: a conical shaped lid that has a steam hole, and a circular base that the cone lid sits over, on hot charcoal. Most tagines for sale outside Morocco are for decorative purposes only, so before purchasing one, check to make sure it's for cooking. Otherwise, a good old fashioned saucepan with a lid usually does the trick. Especially one with a hole in the lid to let out a bit of steam. Serve with couscous and harissa.

2 tbsp olive oil

2 onions, finely chopped

1 tbsp fresh ginger, peeled and finely chopped or grated

4 garlic cloves, finely chopped

1 tsp ground cumin

2 tsp ground coriander

2 tsp paprika

¼ tsp ground cinnamon

½ tsp ground turmeric

¼ tsp cayenne pepper or chilli powder, more to taste

400g tin chopped tomatoes

1 small winter squash or pumpkin (about 700g), peeled, cored and cut into 5cm (2 inch) pieces

200g green lentils

50g dates, finely chopped

1 litre water or vegetable stock

1 preserved lemon, peel only, sliced

salt and pepper

handful of fresh coriander, chopped

handful of fresh parsley, chopped

harissa (optional)

Heat a large saucepan over a medium heat and add the oil. Add the onion and fry for about 5 minutes, or until translucent. While the onion is cooking place all the spices on a plate ready for use.

Add the ginger and garlic to the onions and cook for another minute before adding the spices. Cook the spices off for a minute and then add the tomatoes, squash, lentils, dates, water and lemon peel.

Bring back to a simmering point and continue to cook, uncovered, for a further 30-35 minutes or until the lentils and squash are tender. Taste and adjust the seasoning. Garnish with the fresh chopped coriander and parsley, serve with harissa.

LEMON COUSCOUS *with pomegranate and almonds*

COUSCOUS is the staple carbohydrate in Morocco; it's not a whole grain, but made from semolina (wheat). Moroccan wives used to be chosen on the basis of their couscous steaming ability. Luckily, we have moved on a bit and now all the couscous we buy today has already been steamed. However, I am often asked how to keep couscous from clumping. My reply: reconstitute as directed, then place in a hot oven covered with foil for 10-15 minutes to dry out. This results in light, fluffy couscous that would please anyone.

375ml water

1 tbsp butter

1 tbsp olive oil

½ tsp salt

250g couscous

1 tsp ras el hanout

zest and juice of 1 lemon

50g almonds, toasted and roughly chopped

seeds of ½ pomegranate

10g fresh parsley, roughly chopped

10g fresh coriander, roughly chopped

FOR A VEGAN VERSION
Swap vegan butter or extra virgin olive oil for butter

Preheat the oven to 180°C/Gas Mark 5.

Bring the water to a boil with the butter, oil and salt in a small saucepan. Stir in the couscous, ras el hanout, lemon zest and juice. Take the saucepan off the heat, cover, and set aside until all the water has been absorbed and the couscous is plump, about 5 minutes. Heat a dry frying pan over a medium heat and toast the almonds until fragrant and starting to colour.

Remove the cover from the couscous and fluff with a fork. Transfer the couscous to a baking dish and cover with kitchen foil. Place in the oven for 15 minutes to steam.

To serve, spread the couscous over a large serving platter and sprinkle with the toasted almonds and pomegranate seeds. Garnish the whole dish with chopped flat leaf parsley and coriander.

ORANGE
SINCE 1930
FLEURS D'ORANGE
ماء الزهر
PREMIUM QUALITY
Product of Lebanon
Produit du Liban

COCONUT *and* ORANGE BLOSSOM BISCUITS

AT ABOUT 4:00PM the streets of Marrakesh are flooded with women and their daughters selling treats to tourists and locals alike for afternoon tea. These coconut biscuits were my treat of choice as I love coconut and the hint of orange blossom was an added bonus. Despite being severely overcharged for my first taste, the biscuits still left a sweetness in my mouth.

2 free-range eggs

125g icing sugar

2 tbsp melted butter

2 tbsp oil

1 tsp baking powder

zest of 1 lemon

250g desiccated coconut

80g fine semolina

FOR SHAPING
2 tbsp orange flower water, more if needed

icing sugar

TO SERVE
sliced oranges and dates (optional)

Preheat the oven to 175°C/Gas Mark 4. Lightly oil 2 baking trays.

Beat the eggs with the icing sugar, then add the butter, oil, baking powder, and lemon zest and mix well. Stir in the coconut. Add the semolina and mix to make a moist, crumbly dough which is firm enough to shape into balls. Add more coconut if the dough is not firm enough.

Wet your hands with orange flower water and take enough dough to roll a small ball the size of a golf ball, squeezing the dough first to compact it. Flatten it slightly in your palms to form a thick disc. Roll the disc in icing sugar and place on a greased baking tray. Repeat the process, wetting your hands with orange flower water each time you form a cookie, until all the dough has been shaped.

Bake the cookies for about 15-20 minutes or until golden brown. Transfer to a wire rack to cool. Serve with sliced oranges and dates.

TASTE *of* THAILAND

WHEN IT COMES to choosing from the countries that I've visited Thailand is top of my list. Maybe it's due to the fact I was travelling with my dear friend Sage, whom I rarely see. We gallivanted all over the country visiting temples, getting massages, enjoying the warm sea and devouring the delicious food on offer. Fresh fruit, ripe and dripping with juice, spicy curries, sweet and tangy noodles and fresh salads where daily treats.

While in Chiang Mai we visited an organic farm for a cookery class. It was delightful seeing the green papayas hanging from the trees, picking the fresh herbs to use in the dishes we were about to create and smelling the intoxicating tropical flowers. The day also included a trip to the local market for purchasing ingredients. There we witnessed vats of steaming curry and big pots of curry paste that were far too hot for our Western palates. Recalling such delicious memories makes me want to go back.

Kaffir lime leaves are available in the freezer of most Asian grocery stores. Dry leaves are sold more widely, however, the flavour from frozen is far superior and far better value for money. If you're unable to find kaffir lime leaves substitute with 1 teaspoon of lime zest.

Galangal is commonly found in Thai cookery, it is a rhizome like ginger, however the flavour is very different. Galangal has more of a sharp citrusy, almost piney flavour whereas ginger is pungent and spicy. The two can not really be interchanged. Fresh or frozen galangal is becoming more widely available at supermarkets and can definitely be found at a good Asian market.

Fish sauce is a common ingredient in Thai cuisine, adding a fermented umami kick. There are many vegan fish sauce recipes that can be made, but over the years I have found by adding a little extra lime and soy sauce the desired taste is achieved. Soy sauce or tamari is already a fermented product and lime adds the bitterness. When doing your final tasting for these recipes, take that into consideration.

GALLOPING HORSES
pineapple satay

THESE LITTLE CANAPÉS not only look gorgeous, they are sure to be a crowd pleaser. Easy to make and simple to assemble. The satay sauce can also be used as a sauce or dressing for steamed vegetables.

Roasted winter squash or cauliflower are lovely seasonal alternatives to the more exotic pineapple. Simply preheat the oven to 200°C/Gas Mark 6, cut the veg into 2cm (1 inch) pieces and place on a baking tray. Coat with a bit of oil and roast until tender, about 15-20 minutes.

1 tbsp rapeseed oil

8 small round shallots, thinly sliced

4 tbsp crunchy peanut butter

1 tbsp palm sugar or coconut sugar

2 tbsp soy sauce or 1 tbsp tamari for gluten free

1 small pineapple, peeled and cut into 2.5cm (1 inch) triangles

1 lime

1 large red chilli, sliced into thin rings, seeds optional

handful of coriander leaves

Heat the oil in a frying pan over a medium heat and add the shallots. Pan fry until they're brown, adding a splash of water if they start to stick. Turn the heat down if they start to burn. Reduce the heat and add the peanut butter, sugar and soy sauce. Stir until the sugar has melted. The mixture should be sweet and salty; taste and adjust seasoning.

Arrange the pineapple triangles on a plate and place a heaped teaspoon of the peanut mixture on each. Top each with a squeeze of lime, a coriander leaf and a ring of chilli. Serve with cocktail sticks.

SERVES 4-6

TOM KHA
fragrant coconut, lemongrass and galangal soup

I WAS GOING to a friend's house for dinner and I offered to bring tom kha. When I arrived, my friend was pleasantly surprised that tom kha was a soup and not an extra guest! She now makes this soup all the time.

This is my go to soup when I start feeling under the weather. The heat of the chillies, the fragrant lemongrass and galangal and the creaminess of coconut are just perfect. The soup keeps well for about three days.

FOR THE BROTH

400ml coconut milk

800ml water

3 lemon grass stalks, bashed with the bottom of a knife or a rolling pin to release flavour

5cm (2 inches) galangal, thinly sliced

3 shallots, sliced

FOR THE SOUP

100g shiitake or brown mushrooms, thinly sliced, stems removed if using shiitakes

2 small pak choi or ½ small Chinese cabbage, sliced into small strips

1 medium carrot, peeled and sliced into thin matchsticks

2 medium tomatoes, sliced into wedges

3 kaffir lime leaves, torn to release their flavour

1 tsp palm sugar or coconut sugar

pinch of salt, to taste

1 tbsp soy sauce or ½ tbsp tamari for gluten free

juice of ½ lime, more to taste

25g fresh coriander, roughly chopped, reserve some to garnish

GARNISHES

2 Thai chillies, thinly sliced, more if you like it hotter

2 spring onions, white and green parts, thinly sliced

reserved coriander leaves

To make the broth, put the coconut milk and water into a large saucepan or wok and add the stock. Heat until boiling. Add the lemongrass, galangal and shallot and simmer for at least 15 minutes, 30 minutes if you have time. Pass the broth through a sieve to remove any chunks, pressing gently to extract as much flavour as possible. Return the broth to the saucepan.

To the broth add the mushrooms, pak choi, carrot, tomatoes and lime leaves and continue simmering until cooked, about 10 minutes.

Season with the sugar, salt and soy sauce. Finally, add the lime juice and coriander. Taste and adjust the seasoning, adding more salt, lime juice, sugar, salt or soy sauce, if needed. Thai food should always have a good balance of sweet, salty, sour and spicy. The spicy will come with the addition of the chillies.

To serve, ladle the broth into bowls and garnish with the chillies, spring onions and reserved coriander.

SOM TUM
green papaya salad

GREEN PAPAYA is hands down my favourite Thai dish. Traditionally papaya is used that is picked while still green, long before it's ripe, but a combination of carrot and white cabbage provide a lovely local alternative here in the UK. If you do wish to make it with green papaya check your local Asian grocery store.

A Thai restaurant I frequented while living in Northern California served me a perfectly spicy version of this salad upon my request for some heat. While chatting with the waitress I said that the spice was just the right amount and inquired how many chillies were added. She replied 2, I then asked how many she used when she made it for herself. She replied 8!

75g blanched peanuts, toasted and roughly chopped, reserve 2 tbsp for garnish

1 medium green papaya, about 500g (or 350g carrot and 150g cabbage, grated)

2 small garlic cloves

12 French beans, trimmed and sliced in half or 3 long Thai beans, sliced into 2.5cm (1 inch) pieces

2 green Thai chillies

2 tomatoes, each cut into 6 wedges

2 tbsp fresh lime juice

1 tbsp palm sugar or coconut sugar

1 tbsp soy sauce or ½ tbsp tamari for gluten free

salt, to taste

Preheat the oven to 200°C/Gas Mark 6. Place the peanuts on a dry baking tray. Toast for 5-8 minutes or until turning golden and smelling fragrant. Be sure to move the nuts around the baking tray at least once while toasting. Cool and roughly chop with a knife or food processor.

Peel and grate the green papaya (or carrot and cabbage) and set aside. Using a mortar and pestle (or a metal bowl and the end of a rolling pin) pound the garlic, green beans and chillies, until well smashed. Add the tomatoes and pound a few times just to get the juices out.

In a separate bowl, big enough to toss the salad in, combine the lime juice, sugar and soy sauce.

Add the papaya (or carrots and cabbage), peanuts, and tomato mixture to the bowl. Mix well with a spoon and use the pestle to gently push down and slightly bruise the vegetables. This helps the vegetables to absorb the flavours of the salad.

Taste and adjust the seasoning, adding more chilli for heat, sugar for sweet, lime for sour or salt/soy sauce for saltiness, if needed. Try to achieve a balance of all the flavours. Garnish with the remaining peanuts.

PAD THAI

SERVES 4

OVER THE YEARS, I have tried various Pad Thai recipes and have been gravely disappointed. This recipe is a variation of one I learned in Chang Mai, Thailand. It's truly authentic and delivers all that a vegetarian Pad Thai should.

A couple of times a year I run a Pad Thai noodle bar at my local pub. We usually serve 100 people in about 3 hours leaving me with 'wok arm' a form of tennis elbow. But it's worth it to see all those smiling faces from a simple bowl of noodles. At the noodle bar, and when I make the noodles at home, I always have bowls of extra garnishes and garlic chilli hot sauce for people to pile on.

This recipe calls for sweetened radish or fermented turnip. Despite the name difference they are the same product; long white mouli radish that has been sweetened and fermented is available at Asian markets or online. If you go to a market and have difficulty finding it, ask for the radish used in Pad Thai. It is optional, but it delivers authentic flavour, not a deal breaker, but definitely worth seeking out. It keeps very well for about a year in an airtight container. It is also lovely in an omelette with spring onions topped with garlic chilli sauce.

200g flat rice noodles, 5mm or size L

6 spring onions

3 tbsp rapeseed oil

2 free-range eggs

3 tbsp rapeseed oil

200g firm tofu, chopped into small cubes

2 cloves garlic, finely chopped

30g sweetened radish or fermented turnip (optional), finely chopped

2 green or red Thai chillies, finely chopped, seeds removed for less heat

150g bean sprouts

FOR THE SAUCE

3 tbsp soy sauce or 2 tbsp tamari for gluten free

2 tbsp tamarind concentrate mixed with 200ml warm water

juice of 2 limes

1 tbsp palm sugar or coconut sugar

pinch of chilli powder

pinch of salt

Place the noodles in a large bowl and cover with room temperature water. Let the noodles stand for 30 minutes while you prepare the rest of the ingredients; the noodles are ready when they are soft enough to wrap around your finger. When ready, drain and set aside. This method prevents the noodles from sticking together and creating claggy noodles. The noodles finish cooking in the sauce and result in a lovely plate of noodles instead of a gooey starchy mess.

Preheat the oven to 200°C/Gas Mark 6.

For the garnish place the peanuts on a dry baking tray and toast for 5-8 minutes or until they turn golden and smell fragrant. Be sure to move the nuts around the baking tray at least once while toasting. Cool and roughly chop with a knife or food processor.

Meanwhile, prepare the spring onions by cutting them in half lengthways to separate the white part form the green part. Slice both halves into thin slices lengthways and keep separate. Set aside.

Combine the ingredients for the sauce. Mix well and set aside.

Crack the eggs into a bowl. Heat 1 tablespoon of oil in a wok on a medium-high heat and add the egg to the wok stirring quickly using a large metal spoon or spatula to scramble. Remove the scrambled egg from the wok and set aside.

Add the remaining 1 tablespoon of oil, heat and fry the tofu until golden. Turn the heat down to low, add the remaining oil, garlic, radish and chilli, stirring constantly, until fragrant. This usually takes about 1 minute. Add the sauce mixture and noodles to the wok. Turn the heat up to medium-high.

TO GARNISH
1 lime, sliced into wedges

100g blanched peanuts, toasted and roughly chopped

chilli flakes

FOR A VEGAN VERSION
Omit the eggs and use 100g more tofu

Stir-fry until the noodles are warm and fully cooked. Most of the sauce will be absorbed by the noodles. Add the white part of the spring onion, the cooked egg and most of the bean sprouts. Stir-fry thoroughly until hot and well mixed.

Remove the wok from the heat and toss in the green bits of the spring onion. Plate the stir fry and top with remaining bean sprouts. Garnish with wedges of lime and sprinkle with the peanuts and chilli flakes.

THAI MASSAMAN CURRY *with tofu*

MASSAMAN CURRY is very different to red or green curry in flavour but similar to make. It is generally thought to be a reference to Mussulman, an old form of the word Muslim. However, some believe the recipe came from a Persian merchant, while others think the dish was developed in southern Thailand influenced by Malay and Indian cuisine. Others think the name is derived from the Malay word masam for sour. Regardless how the dish came to be, it's very popular and delicious.

The recipe calls for whole spices to be ground into a powder. Ground spices can also be used, but it will not have the freshness of whole.

TO MAKE THE PASTE

½ tsp cumin seeds

2 tsp coriander seeds

½ tsp black peppercorns

3 whole cloves

1 inch piece cinnamon quill

4 cardamom pods, smash and use seeds only

½ tsp black peppercorns

4 dried red chillies, soaked in water for about 15 minutes, seeds removed

3 shallots, peeled

4 garlic cloves, peeled

5cm (2 inches) galangal, sliced

1 piece fresh lemongrass, white bottom part only, thinly sliced

½ tsp turmeric

¼ tsp nutmeg, freshly grated

¼ tsp salt

TO MAKE THE CURRY

200g tofu

2 tbsp rapeseed oil

the Massaman curry paste you've just made (full amount)

2 tsp palm sugar or coconut sugar

400ml tin of coconut milk

1 tbsp tamarind concentrate

1 onion, sliced

2 medium carrots, peeled and diagonally sliced into 1.25cm (½ inch) wide chunks

2 medium potatoes or sweet potatoes, peeled and cut into 2.5cm (1 inch) cubes

200ml water

75g blanched peanuts or whole cashew nuts

2 tsp soy sauce or 1 tsp tamari for gluten free

2 spring onions, sliced

2 tbsp fresh coriander, chopped

FOR THE PASTE:

Toast the cumin, coriander seeds, peppercorns, cloves, cinnamon, cardamom and soaked chillies in a dry frying pan until fragrant and changing colour, being careful not to burn.

Let the spices cool and grind in a spice grinder or with a mortar and pestle until fine.

In a dry frying pan, dry fry the shallots, garlic, galangal, and lemongrass over a high heat until slightly brown.

Place the spices, toasted shallots, garlic, galangal, and lemongrass, and the remaining ingredients in a food processor or in a jug if using a hand blender. Process until the mixture forms a dry paste. If the mixture is not blending well, add 1 tablespoon of coconut milk, but only as a last resort.

FOR THE CURRY:

Wrap the tofu in a clean tea towel and place a weight on it to release the excess moisture. Leave for 10 minutes, then remove and cut into 1.25cm (1 inch) pieces.

Heat 1 tablespoon of the oil in a frying pan or wok and fry the tofu until golden, about 5-8 minutes. Remove from the pan and set aside. Heat the remaining oil in a saucepan or wok and fry the curry paste for 1 minute. Add the sugar, ¼ tin of coconut milk, tamarind and the onion, carrot and potatoes. Simmer for 5 minutes.

Add the remaining coconut milk and water, and bring to the boil. Reduce the heat and simmer until the vegetables are nearly tender, about 10 minutes. Add the fried tofu and peanuts and simmer for a further 5 minutes.

Now add the soy sauce or tamari and mix well. Taste the curry and adjust the seasoning if necessary. It should taste a bit spicy, creamy, sweet and salty.

Serve with jasmine rice and garnish with spring onions and coriander.

THAI GREEN CURRY
with green jackfruit

GREEN JACKFRUIT is a great vegetarian alternative in curry. It has a great texture and absorbs the full flavours in the sauce. It's sold in Asian markets or online. Make sure that you are purchasing the young green jackfruit in brine, not ripe and yellow in syrup. Pan fried tofu or tempeh can also be used.

Many vegetables taste great in curries, so swap and change depending on what's in season. Carrots, squash, broccoli, cauliflower, courgette, aubergine, potato and asparagus are a few suggestions.

When going to the trouble of making your own curry paste, double or triple the paste recipe, divide and freeze the remaining batches for a quick meal another time.

TO MAKE THE PASTE

½ tsp cumin seeds

½ tsp coriander seeds

4 long green chillies, seeds removed and chopped

3 small round shallots

3 garlic cloves, peeled

2 kaffir lime leaves

5cm (2 inch) piece of galangal sliced

2 tsp lime zest (keep the juice for the curry)

2 pieces of fresh lemongrass, bottom white bit only, thinly sliced

20g fresh coriander

¼ tsp black pepper

¼ tsp salt

TO MAKE THE CURRY

1 tbsp rapeseed oil

the Thai green curry paste you have just made (full amount)

2 tsp palm sugar or coconut sugar

400ml coconut milk

1 onion, sliced

1 red pepper, cut into 2.5cm (1 inch) pieces

100g mushrooms, quartered or smaller if large

100g French bean, stems removed and sliced into 5cm (2 inch) pieces

200ml water

565g tin green jackfruit, drained, rinsed and cut into 1.25cm (½ inch) pieces

2 tsp soy sauce or 1 tsp tamari for gluten free

4 kaffir lime leaves,

25 leaves of Thai basil, torn

salt to taste

FOR THE PASTE:

Toast the cumin and coriander seeds in a dry frying pan until fragrant, being careful not to burn.

Place the remaining ingredients, including the toasted cumin and coriander seeds, into a food processor or blender. Process until the mixture forms a dry paste. If the mixture is not blending well add 1 tablespoon of coconut milk, but only as a last resort.

FOR THE CURRY:

Heat the oil in a medium sized saucepan and sauté the curry paste for 1 minute. Add the sugar, 100ml of the coconut milk and the onion, red pepper, mushrooms, and French beans. Simmer for 5 minutes.

Add the remaining coconut milk and water, and bring to the boil. Reduce the heat and simmer until the vegetables are nearly tender, about 10 minutes. Add the green jackfruit and cook for 5 more minutes.

Next, stir in the soy sauce, lime leaves and Thai basil. Taste and adjust the seasoning. It should be a bit spicy, creamy, sweet and salty. The juice of the zested lime can also be added. Serve with jasmine rice.

SERVES 4-6

PINEAPPLE FRIED RICE

PINEAPPLE FRIED RICE is one of my favourite Thai dishes. Slightly lesser known than the likes of pad Thai or green curry, it's fresh, fruity, nutritious and so delicious. Easy to do, impressive when served in the fresh pineapple and a good use of leftover rice.

1 small pineapple or 1 large tin of pineapple chunks

2 tbsp rapeseed oil

500g cooked rice, or about 200g uncooked rice

2 small round shallots, finely chopped

20g ginger, peeled and grated or finely chopped

3 garlic cloves, finely chopped

2 small green or red Thai chillies, thinly sliced, seeds removed for less heat

1 free-range egg (optional)

1 carrot, peeled and grated

75g peas, thawed if frozen or fresh

75g cashew nuts or cashew pieces, toasted

FOR THE SAUCE

2 tbsp soy sauce or 1 tbsp tamari for gluten free

2 tsp curry powder

1 tsp palm sugar or coconut sugar

1 lime, juice only

GARNISHES

fresh coriander

2 spring onions, white and green parts, finely chopped

FOR A VEGAN VERSION

Omit the egg and use 100g fried tofu instead

Cut the unpeeled pineapple in half lengthways and scoop out the fruit. Cut the fruit into bite sized chunks. Reserve the pineapple shell for serving the rice in.

Mix 1 tablespoon of oil with the cooked rice, using your fingers to separate any grains that are stuck together and set aside. Mix the sauce ingredients together.

Heat a wok or frying pan over a medium-high heat. Add the remaining oil and fry the shallots, ginger, garlic and chillies until fragrant, about 1 minute. Whenever the wok becomes a little dry, add 1 tablespoon of water. Crack the egg into the wok if using and stir quickly to scramble. Add the carrot and peas and stir-fry for 1-2 minutes, adding more water if needed.

Add the cooked rice, pineapple chunks and cashews to the wok. Drizzle the sauce mixture in and gently stir-fry over a medium to high heat until the rice starts popping, usually about 5-8 minutes. If the ingredients start to stick, add a splash of water, not too much as the rice will get soggy and fall apart.

Remove from the heat, taste and adjust the seasoning. Serve in the scooped out pineapple and garnish with fresh coriander and chopped spring onions.

MAKES 6 INDIVIDUAL RAMEKINS OR 1 X 23CM (9 INCH) CAKE.

THAI STYLE CRÈME CARAMEL *with mango*

THIS RECIPE is very similar to crème brûlée but made with coconut milk for a Thai twist. This is a delicious and simple pudding, great for dinner parties as it can be made in advance and chilled in the fridge until you are ready to serve.

rapeseed or coconut oil for greasing

6 tbsp maple syrup or golden syrup

3 free-range eggs

pinch of salt

2 tbsp sugar

1 tsp vanilla extract

400g tinned coconut milk

GARNISHES

fresh mango, peeled and thinly sliced

Thai basil

FOR A VEGAN VERSION

Simply omit the eggs and instead mix 1 tablespoon of agar agar flakes with 150ml water, salt, sugar, vanilla and coconut milk. Gently boil for 5 minutes, then pour into prepared ramekins and chill, no need to bake.

Preheat the oven to 170°C/Gas Mark 4-5. Lightly grease the ramekins with oil and pour 1 tablespoon of maple syrup in each.

Beat the eggs with an electric beater or by hand with a whisk for at least 1 minute, until fluffy. Add the salt, sugar, vanilla and coconut milk to the eggs and whisk until well blended.

Divide the coconut mixture between the ramekins (do not stir, the syrup will naturally remain at the bottom of the ramekin). Place the ramekins in a large glass baking dish or deep-sided roasting pan. Pour hot water into the bottom of the baking dish or pan; the water should reach at least half way up the side of the ramekins. Bake for 30 minutes, or until a fork inserted into the pudding comes out clean. Allow to cool then place in the refrigerator until ready to serve.

To remove from the ramekins, simply submerge the ramekin in hot water for 15-30 seconds, then run a knife around the edge and invert over individual dessert plates to release. The pudding should fall out easily, with the syrup naturally dripping down over the coconut custard.

Garnish with fresh sliced mango and Thai basil.

WORLD STREET FOOD

STREET FOOD is usually finger food or eaten out of a disposable container. It's quick, cheaper than restaurant food and full of flavour. Every country and every city has its own version. Lately we've seen the tradition change, with street food trucks rocking up on busy city streets during lunchtime and with quickly forming queues eager for the freshest, tastiest bites on offer.

Historically, when travelling, people were often told to avoid street food because of the risk of contamination or spread of food-borne diseases. Studies have proven that incidents like these are extremely low compared with those in a traditional restaurant setting. This is mainly due to the fact the food is freshly made and eaten right away, not stored. Whenever I'm travelling, I always try the street food. Take a good look around and find where the locals are eating. It's often the place to go.

SWEETCORN EMPANADAS

THE ORIGINAL orientation of empanadas is under debate, but these filled pastries can be found in Portugal, Spain and various parts of South America. Like the Cornish pasty, a cooked filling is wrapped inside pastry and then cooked. Empanadas can be both sweet and savoury.

This recipe has a sweetcorn filling but feel free to alter depending on what's in season. To make beetroot and feta, simply cook the beetroot like a jacket potato, peel and grate, then crumble the feta and mix well before filling the empanada. Winter squash and black bean is also a tasty alternative. Just roast the winter squash until tender, mash with a fork and mix in the black beans and season with a bit of smoked paprika and cumin.

This pastry recipe is made using hot water and is extremely forgiving. For those that are daunted by pastry, this is a great recipe to try. I specify frozen or fresh sweetcorn, but not tinned; coming from a part of America where we only eat fresh corn on the cob the day it's picked, I have a severe dislike for the tinned stuff. Up to you though, if it's easier and you like it, go for it.

FOR THE DOUGH

225ml water

100g butter

350g plain flour

½ tsp salt

¼ tsp paprika

FOR THE FILLING

500g sweetcorn, fresh removed from cob or thawed frozen

6 spring onions, thinly sliced

1 tbsp oil

3 cloves garlic, finely chopped

60ml single cream or milk

juice of half a lime, more if needed

1 tsp smoked or regular paprika

salt and pepper to taste

100g grated mild cheese

1 free-range egg, beaten

1 tbsp water

VE

To make the pastry heat the water and butter in a medium pot over a medium heat until the butter has melted. Turn off the heat if it begins to boil, allowing to sit until melted. Don't boil as this evaporates the water. Mix the flour, salt and paprika in a large mixing bowl and make a well in the centre.

Pour in the liquid and carefully work the flour into the dough first using a rubber spatula then with your hands when it is cool enough to touch, until you get a wet, oily dough. Wrap the pastry in clingfilm and refrigerate for at least 2 hours.

To make the filling place a frying pan on a medium heat and cook the sweetcorn and spring onions in oil for about 3 minutes. Add the garlic, milk, lime juice, paprika, salt and pepper and cook for 5 more minutes until the sweetcorn is soft. In a food processor, pulse 3-4 times until the mixture is uniform, but leaving a few sweetcorn kernels whole. Leave to cool then stir in the cheese.

To assemble the empanadas preheat the oven to 200°C/Gas Mark 6. Grease two baking trays, or line with parchment paper. Whisk the egg and water together in a small bowl to make an egg wash.

Divide the dough into 12 large or 24 small balls. Using a rolling pin, roll out the dough balls on a well-floured surface into circles that are about 1/3 inch thick (not too thin!).

Place 1-3 tablespoons (depending on which size you are making) of filling in the centre of each dough circle. Fold over and press the edges firmly to seal, starting from the middle and working out to the edges. To make the 'rope' around the edge, pinch 1.25cm (½ inch) of one corner edge between your thumb and index finger and fold the edge over onto itself. Pinch and pull another 1.25cm (½ inch) of the edge and fold again, making a rough triangle over the first fold. Repeat this folding around the edge, pressing each fold tightly.

Place the empanadas on the prepared baking trays and brush with the egg wash. Bake for 15-20 minutes for small and 20-25 minutes for large, or until golden brown.

FOR A VEGAN VERSION

Make the pastry with vegan butter. For the filling, use non-dairy milk or cream and substitute cheese with vegan cheese or 3 tablespoons of nutritional yeast. Brush with melted vegan margarine or non-dairy milk instead of egg.

Alternatively, the empanadas can be deep fried and this is how they are traditionally served - needless to say the results are delicious! Skip the egg wash, heat plenty of oil in a large frying pan or wok to 175°C and spoon the oil over the empanadas while cooking until the pasty is golden and bubbly.

SAMOSAS
with fresh mint and coriander chutney

EVERYONE LOVES a good samosa. This recipe makes a bundle of the little parcels, but don't worry if they're not gobbled up because they freeze well too. The secret to this recipe is the amchoor powder, which is a fruity spice powder made from dried green mangos. It provides a citrusy seasoning and is readily available in world food shops. Lemon juice can be used instead. The mint chutney recipe is fresh, punchy and a great accompaniment to these samosas or any Indian dish. It's also really easy to make.

FOR THE FILLING
500g potatoes

3 tbsp oil - sunflower, rapeseed, coconut or ghee

½ tsp mustard seeds

1 small onion, finely chopped

1 tsp ginger, finely chopped

100g fresh or frozen peas

1 tbsp ground coriander

2 tsp ground cumin

¼ tsp red chilli powder

1 tsp garam masala

1½ tsp amchoor, or juice of ½ lemon

salt, to taste

splash of water

4 tbsp fresh coriander, finely chopped

FOR THE PASTRY
500g plain flour

2 tsp nigella seeds, optional

1 tsp salt

8 tbsp rapeseed oil, coconut oil or ghee

200ml water

Boil the potatoes in a saucepan of salted water for 20-25 minutes, or until tender, then drain. When cool enough to handle, grate or put through a potato ricer.

To make the pastry, mix the flour, nigella seeds and salt in a bowl. Make a well in the centre and add the oil and enough water to make a firm dough (you may not need all the water). Knead the dough on a floured surface until smooth and roll into a ball. Cover in clingfilm and set aside at room temperature for 30 minutes.

Heat the oil in a small non-stick pan and fry the mustard seeds for about 10 seconds or until they begin to splutter. Add the onion and ginger and cook for 2-3 minutes over a high heat. Add the peas, stir well and add the spices, amchoor, salt and a splash of water (if using lemon juice instead of amchoor, add this instead of the water). Cook for 1-2 minutes, then add the cooked potatoes and fresh coriander and cook for 2-3 more minutes. Taste and adjust the seasoning.

To make the samosas, cut the dough into six even-sized pieces for larger samosas or 12 even size pieces for smaller and roll into balls. Use a rolling pin to roll each ball into a thin circle, about 15cm (6 inch) diameter. Cut each circle in half to form two semicircles.

Take a semicircle, brush the edges with water to seal and fold into a cone by lifting the bottom edge of the cut side across to the middle of the round side. Fill the cone about half-full with the samosa filling then fold the remaining pastry over to create a triangle, press tightly to seal. Repeat with the remaining dough and filling.

Heat the oil in a deep fat fryer or deep wok to 190°C/Gas Mark 5. Fry in the hot oil, spooning oil over the top and turning over until golden, and bubbles appear. Drain on kitchen towels. Alternatively, the samosas can be baked. Brush with an egg wash or melted butter or coconut oil and place on a baking tray. Bake in a preheated oven at 200°C/Gas Mark 6 for 15 minutes or until golden.

Samosa wrappers or filo dough can also be used to make samosas. The wrappers can be found in the freezer at world food shops.

MAKES 250ML

MINT & CORIANDER CHUTNEY

1 bunch fresh mint, leaves only
1 bunch fresh coriander
2 garlic cloves
2.5 cm (1 inch) piece of ginger
2 green chillies, deseeded
2 tsp sugar
½ tsp salt
juice of ½ a lime, more to taste

GF VE

Prepare the fresh herbs by removing all the mint leaves from their stems and removing and discarding the bottom third of the coriander stems.

Peel the garlic and ginger and remove the seeds from the green chillies. Grind these and all the other ingredients into a smooth paste in a food processor or using a hand blender. Chill and serve.

VIETNAMESE RICE PAPER ROLLS

with lime and chilli dipping sauce (Nuoc Mam Cham)

VIETNAMESE rice paper rolls are not fried, they are served fresh. Rice paper is soaked and packed with fresh herbs, vegetables and rice noodles and served with a gorgeous dipping sauce to create an explosion of taste. These work great as an interactive starter for a dinner party. The fillings can be prepared in advance and the guests can roll their own.

The spring rolls are best served on the day they are made and do not freeze well, but can be made a few hours in advance and stored in the fridge. Other fillings include fresh mango, smoked tofu, sugar snap pea pods or finely shredded cabbage.

50g rice or mung bean vermicelli noodles

6-8 lettuce leaves, finely shredded

50g beansprouts

2 carrots, peeled and grated or sliced into fine julienne

1 ripe avocado, halved, stone removed and sliced

fresh coriander, left whole

fresh Thai basil leaves, removed from stem

fresh mint leaves, removed from stem

toasted peanuts or cashews, roughly chopped

1 pack of rice paper wraps

FOR THE LIME AND CHILLI DIPPING SAUCE
1 tbsp grated palm sugar or brown sugar

4 tbsp hot water

1 garlic clove, peeled and finely chopped

1 small red or green chilli, deseeded and finely chopped

2 tbsp soy sauce or 1 tbsp tamari for gluten free

juice of 1 lime

Bring a small saucepan of water to a boil and add the noodles, remove from the heat and leave to soak for 5 minutes. Drain and rinse, allow to cool. Prepare the lettuce, bean sprouts, carrots, avocado and fresh herbs and place in individual bowls or separate piles on a plate or chopping board. Do not combine; the idea is to have lots of little bowls/piles of filling ingredients.

For the dipping sauce, stir the sugar into the hot water until it dissolves. Combine the remaining ingredients and mix well.

Place the rice paper wraps in a bowl of water, one at a time, for 15-30 seconds or until it becomes pliable, but not totally soft. Place the wrap onto a dry towel. Place 2-3 stems or leaves of each herb about 2.5cm (1 inch) from the bottom of the wrap. Top with a slice of avocado then add a small amount each of rice noodles, lettuce, beansprouts, carrot and chopped peanuts. Bring the bottom of the wrap up until it covers all the vegetables, then fold the sides in and continue rolling up as tightly as possible. The rice paper is quite forgiving. Place on a plate with the seam facing down to seal.

To serve, either leave whole or slice the rolls in half using a serrated knife. Place with one resting on the other, cut side up. Serve with the dipping sauce either on the plate or in a small ramekin.

MALAYSIAN TOFU & AUBERGINE SATAY

SATAY HAS BECOME very well-known and there are lots of variations of the sauce served with the skewers. This satay sauce is quite authentic and uses peanuts instead of peanut butter to obtain a crunchy texture. The skewers can be cooked under the grill, in the oven or on the barbeque.

This recipe calls for tofu and aubergine, but most vegetables and seiten (wheat meat) or tempeh (fermented soya bean cake) can also be used. Cauliflower is pretty spectacular when used in this recipe.

Kecap manis is an Indonesian sweet soy sauce widely available at all major grocery stores. If you can't find it, 2 teaspoons of soy sauce and 1 teaspoon of molasses or brown sugar equals 1 tablespoon of kecap manis. For a gluten free version use 1 ½ tsp tamari instead of the soy sauce.

400g firm tofu

1 large aubergine

bamboo skewers (soaked in water for 1 hour to avoid burning if using the grill or barbecue)

1 cucumber

FOR THE MARINADE
2 lemongrass stalks, white parts only

6 small or 3 large shallots, peeled

2 garlic cloves, peeled

2 tbsp rapeseed, sunflower or vegetable oil

½ tsp chilli powder

1 tsp turmeric powder

1 tbsp ground coriander

1 tsp ground cumin

2 tbsp kecap manis (see top of recipe for gluten free)

juice of ½ lime

FOR THE SATAY SAUCE
125g blanched peanuts, toasted

2 tbsp rapeseed, sunflower or vegetable oil

125ml water

1 tbsp kecap manis (see top of recipe for gluten free)

2 tsp palm sugar or demerara sugar

⅛ tsp salt

1 heaped tbsp tamarind concentrate mixed with 60ml hot water

150ml coconut milk

FOR THE SPICE PASTE
3-4 dried red chillies, seeds removed and soaked in warm water

1 garlic clove

2 shallots

1 lemongrass stalk, white parts only

1.25cm (½ inch) galangal or ginger

1 tbsp ground coriander

Remove the tofu from its packaging, wrap in a tea towel and put a weight on top to remove any excess moisture and leave for 10-15 minutes. Soak the chillies in warm water for about 15 minutes.

Preheat the oven to 180°C/Gas Mark 4. To make the marinade, combine all the marinade ingredients in a blender, or a jug if using a hand blender, and blend well.

Cut the tofu into 1.25cm (½ inch) cubes. Slice the aubergine into 1.25cm (½ inch) cubes. Place the tofu, aubergines and marinade in a large bowl and mix well. Cover and leave for at least one hour.

To make the sauce, toast the peanuts in the oven for 5-10 minutes or until fragrant and golden, be careful not to burn. Then crush the peanuts coarsely with a mortar and pestle or mini food processor and set aside. Turn the oven off until ready to cook the satay.

Chop the spice paste ingredients and blend until fine with a hand blender or mini food processor. Heat the oil in a pan and fry the spice paste until aromatic and spicy smelling. Be careful not to inhale as it will make you cough!

Add the peanuts, kecap manis, sugar, salt, tamarind and coconut milk and stir thoroughly. Simmer on a low heat and continue stirring for about 3 minutes. If the sauce is too thick, add a bit of water. Taste and adjust the seasoning.

Now to make the skewers. Preheat the oven to 200°C/Gas Mark 6 or the grill/barbecue to high - just remember to soak the skewers in water first if using the grill or barbecue. Assemble the skewers by impaling the marinated aubergine and tofu.

If using the oven, bake on a greased baking tray until the vegetables are tender, about 30 minutes, turning once half way through. Grill/barbecue under a high heat for 8 minutes on each side, or until tender and starting to colour.

When the satay is cooked, transfer to plates and top with about half the satay sauce. Serve the skewers with the remaining satay sauce and some sliced cucumber.

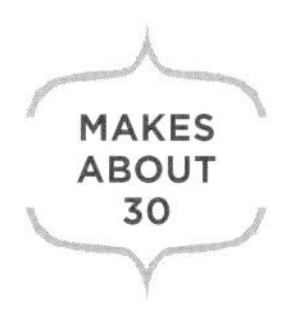

CHINESE CABBAGE & SHIITAKE GYOZA

(Japanese dumplings, also known as pot stickers)

JAPANESE GYOZA dumplings are pan fried and then steamed to create multiple textures in one bite. The filling uses a combination of Chinese cabbage and shiitake mushrooms which provide a wonderful texture to the filling and a deep flavour. The wrappers are easily found in the freezer section of most world foods shops. This recipe makes quite a few of these tasty dumplings, but they can be frozen before cooking and then cooked from frozen. Simply place the assembled dumplings on a tray lined with baking paper and freeze. Once frozen, transfer into a freezer bag and seal shut.

Remember to take your time slicing the vegetables as the final product is quite small. Although a bit of shrinkage occurs when cooking the vegetables for the filling, large pieces will be difficult to work with and potentially poke through the gyoza skins.

FOR THE DIPPING SAUCE
3 tbsp soy sauce or
1 ½ tbsp tamari

1 tsp toasted sesame oil

1 tbsp rice vinegar

2 tsp ginger, finely grated

1 spring onion, finely sliced

FOR THE PASTRY
1 tbsp oil - rapeseed, sunflower or vegetable

2 carrots, peeled and grated

½ small Chinese cabbage, very finely chopped

100g shiitake or brown mushrooms, very finely chopped

3 spring onions, sliced

2 garlic cloves, finely chopped

2.5cm (1 inch) fresh ginger, finely grated

1 tsp toasted sesame oil

1 tbsp soy sauce or ½ tbsp tamari

oil for frying - rapeseed, sunflower or vegetable

1 pack of round gyoza skins, also called dumplings or pot stickers

To make the dipping sauce, combine all the sauce ingredients in a bowl and stir. Let down with a bit of water if it is too strong.

To make the gyoza filling, heat a frying pan and add the oil. Add the carrot, cabbage and mushrooms and cook for 5-8 minutes or until the vegetables are tender, moving them around the pan regularly. Add the spring onions, garlic, ginger, sesame oil and soy sauce. Cook for another couple of minutes. Remove from the heat and allow to cool.

Place a heaped teaspoon of filling in the middle of a wrapper. Fold the gyoza wrapper by lifting either side of the wrapper up and pinching at the top to create a flat bottom. Pinch the edges together to crimp or pleat to seal it shut.

Cook the gyozas in batches. Heat a small amount of oil in a large frying pan or wok. When the oil is ready, carefully add the dumplings, flat bottom down, and cook on a high heat until golden brown (about 1 minute). Without turning the dumplings over, add 60ml of water to the pan and cover with a lid. Reduce the heat to low and steam the dumplings. Check the dumplings after 2 minutes. When the wrappers appear slightly translucent continue to cook until all the water has evaporated, about 2 minutes. Once you hear a sizzling sound, shake the pan. The dumplings should slide about. If they seem to stick move the pan away from the hob and replace the lid for a moment. Remove the dumplings from the pan with a rubber spatula. If you like, flip them over so the seared surface faces up. Cook the remaining dumplings the same way.

MAKES ABOUT 12

ACARAJE *with salada fresca*

ACARAJE is traditionally encountered in Brazil's north eastern state of Bahia. These falafel type discs are made from black-eyed beans that are soaked, rubbed to remove the skins, then fried. Once the balls are cooked, they are then sliced and filled. This vegetarian version of the authentic street food uses a fresh tomato and avocado salad for the filling. They are delicious!

FOR THE ACARAJE
350g black-eyed beans, soaked overnight

1 small onion

2 garlic cloves

1 tsp ground cumin

¼ - ½ tsp chilli powder

freshly ground black pepper

1 tsp baking powder

1 tsp salt

sunflower or rapeseed oil for frying

FOR THE FRESH SALAD FILLING
2 tbsp olive oil

1 tbsp vinegar

juice of 1 lemon or lime

1 ripe avocado, cut into small cubes

3 ripe tomatoes, seeds removed and cut into small cubes

4 spring onions, thinly sliced

1 green or red chilli, seeds removed, finely chopped

3-4 tbsp fresh coriander, finely chopped

Soak the beans overnight in plenty of water. Rub the beans together between your hands while still in the water to remove the skins. Try to get as many of the skins off as possible, but they do not all have to come off. Drain, rinse and repeat. The skins should float to the top and come off when drained. Don't worry too much if this is a hassle, I have skipped the process and still had good results.

Combine the beans and remaining acaraje ingredients in a blender or food processor. Process the mixture until it forms a thick, smooth paste. The batter should be well blended and hold its shaped when formed.

Heat 5cm (2 inch) of oil in a wok, heavy saucepan or deep fat fryer. While the oil is heating, shape the batter into 5cm (2 inch) wide disc shaped fritters.

Fry the fritters in batches, turning once, until dark golden brown. Carefully remove the fritters from the hot oil with a slotted spoon, and place them on paper towels to cool slightly.

To make the salad, combine the oil, vinegar and lemon/lime juice in a bowl and mix together. Stir in the avocado, tomato, spring onion, chilli and coriander. Season well with salt and pepper. Make a slit in the ball to create an opening, being careful not to go all the way through, and spoon the salada fresca inside. Serve warm.

BANANA FRITTERS

MY FIRST EXPERIENCE with banana fritters was while staying on Koh Phi Phi in Thailand. Our resort was on a private bay and had a restaurant and bar that provided meals and drinks. We ordered the banana fritters on the first night, and every night after. This recipe produces light, crispy, divine fritters that make a special treat or a simple pudding. The batter is also gluten free.

175g white rice flour

30g tapioca flour or cornflour

40g grated palm sugar or brown sugar

½ tsp salt

45g desiccated coconut

250ml water

6-8 bananas

sunflower or rapeseed oil for frying

honey or golden syrup for drizzling

In a medium bowl, mix the rice flour, tapioca flour, sugar, salt and coconut. Stir in the water, a little at a time and mix to form a batter. Let the batter sit for a few minutes; if it's too thick, add a bit more water.

Peel the bananas and cut each into 3 or 4 long pieces. Heat the oil in a deep fat fryer or deep wok to 190°C/Gas Mark 5.

Completely coat each banana in batter then fry in the hot oil until deeply golden. Drain on kitchen towels. Serve immediately drizzled with honey or golden syrup. Chocolate sauce is also delicious.

RECIPE INDEX

MAINS

SIDES

BREADS

PUDDINGS

INDEX

Acknowledgements

NEIL BAKER first and foremost I would like to acknowledge my husband and my best friend. Without him this book would not be a reality. He is my chief taster and biggest support in everything I do. Thank you Neil, I love you with all of my heart.

AMBER HEATH for always encouraging me, being positive and inspiring me to strive to be a good role model for you.

HOLLY MOORE for giving me the reins of the kitchen at Woodruffs Organic Cafe when I was fresh off the plane from America. And for providing me with a place to start the Natural Cookery School.

LAURA KING for your help with the book in its early stages, bookkeeping, chopping, peeling, pot washing, overall great assistance and calmness.

RODDA THOMAS AND RUAN CASTELLINI for hosting Meat Free Mondays at the one and only Crown and Sceptre in Stroud for over 5 years, helping me to share my food with the masses.

WENDY MILNER for all of the beautiful art work and graphic design that you have created for me.

SAM URQUHART my fab behind the scenes web wizard.

KATE LEWIS for hosting Asparagasm supper clubs, Meat Free Mondays in Tetbury, taking me to London for an unforgettable two night run of the Pan Asian Express in Shoreditch and your solid encouragement and contagious creativity.

HILARY CHESTER-MASTER for the trust and freedom you gave when taking me on freelance to teach classes at your utterly amazing The Organic Farm Shop.

YVETTE FARRELL for your support and encouragement over the years and providing me a fabulous place to teach over at Harts Barn Cookery School.

FOODWORKS COOKERY SCHOOL years ago I received a call out of the blue asking me to teach a course in your beautiful venue. This was the start of my freelance chef tutor career.

AMY PITT for all of your help with editing this book, my website, all of those submissions, lovely conversation on dog walks and your enthusiasm for all I do.

MIKE RUGGIER your talented photography has put this book in another league. Thank you for all of the laughs, photos and your patience with my obsession for edible flowers.

IMOGEN SHAW for the fabulous design of the book, racing to meet deadlines and being more than pleasant every step of the way.

ROD SHAW for your number crunching, printer negotiating and reassurance that I will sell the books.

LUCINDA you may not have helped with this book very much, but you have helped me in so many other ways. Thank you for being an excellent assistant and my biggest fan over the last few years.

AMI AND ROB for storing and distributing all of my books.

Big thank you to all of my pot washers, kitchen assistants, helpers, employers, employees and teachers along the way. Each and every one of you has contributed to my life and this book in one way or another.

And lastly to all of my customers that have attended my classes and eaten my food at supper clubs, banquets and events, you inspire me to be the best I can be.

Notes

Notes

Notes

Notes

Erin Baker founded The Natural Cookery School in 2007. What started as a mobile venture now has a permanent home in the old milling town of Nailsworth, Gloucestershire. Here you'll find Erin and her team in a beautiful culinary space, just ripe for cooking classes, dining and events.

PROUDLY MADE IN STROUD